DEMOCRACY

KETER BOOKS

This book is compiled from material originally published in the *Encyclopaedia Judaica*

Copyright © 1974, Keter Publishing House Jerusalem Ltd.
P.O.Box 7145, Jerusalem, Israel

Cat. No. 25066

ISBN 0 7065 1330 4

Printed by Keterpress Enterprises, Jerusalem
Printed in Israel

CONTENTS

CONTRIBUTORS

Moshe Avidor, former ambassador and director general of Israel Academy of Sciences and Humanities

Henry E. Baker, B.C.L., LL.B.: president of District Court, Jerusalem; Research Fellow in Law Faculty, Hebrew University of Jerusalem

Leon Boim, Ph.D.: Associate Professor of Political Sciences, Tel Aviv University

Edwin Emanuel Gutman, Ph.D.: Senior Lecturer in Political Science, Hebrew University of Jerusalem

Chaim Herzog, LL.B.: Major-General (Res.), Israel Defense Forces: military commentator and business executive, Tel Aviv

Yehudah Levanon, Ministry of Absorption, Jerusalem

Arye Levavi, M.A.: ambassador, Ministry for Foreign Affairs, Jerusalem

Misha Louvish, writer and journalist, Jerusalem

Shulamit Nardi, Instructor in English and Contemporary Jewry, Hebrew University of Jerusalem

Chana Palti, Jerusalem

Moshe Rosetti, former Clerk of the Knesset, Tel Aviv

Edwin Samuel, Second Viscount Samuel, C.M.G., B.A.: Emeritus Senior Lecturer in British Institutions, the Hebrew University of Jerusalem: Principal of the Israel Institute of Public Administration, Jerusalem

Geoffrey Wigoder, D.Phil.: Editor in Chief of the *Encyclopaedia Judaica;* the Institute for Contemporary Jewry, the Hebrew University of Jerusalem

DECLARATION OF INDEPENDENCE

IN THE LAND OF ISRAEL the Jewish people came into being. In this Land was shaped their spiritual, religious, and national character. Here they lived in sovereign independence. Here they created a culture of national and universal import, and gave to the world the eternal Book of Books.

Exiled by force, still the Jewish people kept faith with their Land in all the countries of their dispersion, steadfast in their prayer and hope to return and here revive their political freedom.

Fired by this attachment of history and tradition, the Jews in every generation strove to renew their roots in the ancient homeland, and in recent generations they came home in their multitudes.

Veteran pioneers and defenders, and newcomers braving blockade, they made the wilderness bloom, revived their Hebrew tongue, and built villages and towns. They founded a thriving society, master of its own economy and culture, pursuing peace but able to defend itself, bringing the blessing of progress to all the inhabitants of the Land, dedicated to the attainment of sovereign independence.

In 1897 the First Zionist Congress met at the call of Theodor Herzl, seer of the vision of the Jewish State, and gave public voice to the right of the Jewish people to national restoration in their Land.

This right was acknowledged in the Balfour Declaration on 2 November, 1917, and confirmed in the Mandate of the League of Nations, which accorded international validity to the historical connection between the Jewish people and the Land of Israel, and to their right to re-establish their National Home.

The holocaust that in our time destroyed millions of Jews in Europe again proved beyond doubt the compelling need to solve the problem of Jewish homelessness and dependence by the renewal of the Jewish State in the Land of Israel, which would open wide the gates of the homeland to every Jew and endow the Jewish people with the status of a nation with equality of rights within the family of nations.

Despite every hardship, hindrance and peril, the remnant that survived the grim Nazi slaughter in Europe, together with Jews from other countries, pressed on with their exodus to the Land of Israel and continued to assert their right to a life of dignity, freedom and honest toil in the homeland of their people.

In the Second World War, the Jewish community in the Land of Israel played its full part in the struggle of the nations championing freedom and peace against the Nazi forces of evil. Its war effort and the lives of its soldiers won it the right to be numbered among the founding peoples of the United Nations.

On 29 November 1947, the General Assembly of the United Nations adopted a resolution calling for the establishment of a Jewish State in the Land of Israel, and required the inhabitants themselves to take all measures necessary on their part to carry out the resolution. This recognition by the United Nations of the right of the Jewish people to establish their own State is irrevocable.

It is the natural right of the Jewish people, like any other people, to control their own destiny in their sovereign State.

ACCORDINGLY WE, the members of the National Council, representing the Jewish people in the Land of Israel and the Zionist Movement, have assembled on the day of the termination of the British Mandate for Palestine, and by virtue of our natural and historic right and of the resolution of the General Assembly of the United Nations, do hereby proclaim the establishment of a Jewish State in the Land of Israel—the State of Israel.

WE RESOLVE that from the moment the Mandate ends, at midnight on the Sabbath, the sixth of Iyar 5708, the fifteenth day of May 1948, until the establishment of the duly elected authorities of the State in accordance with a Constitution to be adopted by the Elected Constituent Assembly not later than 1 October 1948, the National Council shall act as the Provisional Council of State, and its executive arm, the National Administration, shall constitute the Provisional Government of the Jewish State, and the name of that State shall be Israel.

THE STATE OF ISRAEL will be open to Jewish immigration and the ingathering of exiles. It will devote itself to developing the Land for the good of all its inhabitants.

It will rest upon foundations of liberty, justice and peace as envisioned by the Prophets of Israel. It will maintain complete equality of social and political rights for all its citizens, without distinction of creed, race or sex. It will guarantee freedom of religion and conscience, of language, education and culture. It will safeguard the Holy Places of all religions. It will be loyal to the principles of the United Nations Charter.

THE STATE OF ISRAEL will be prepared to cooperate with the organs and representatives of the United Nations in carrying out the General Assembly resolution of 29 November 1947, and will work for the establishment of the economic union of the whole Land of Israel.

WE APPEAL to the United Nations to assist the Jewish people in the building of their State, and to admit the State of Israel into the family of nations.

EVEN AMIDST the violent attacks launched against us for months past, we call upon the sons of the Arab people dwelling in Israel to keep the peace and to play their part in building the State on the basis of full and equal citizenship and due representation in all its institutions, provisional and permanent.

WE EXTEND the hand of peace and good-neighbourliness to all the States around us and to their peoples, and we call upon them to cooperate in mutual helpfulness with the independent Jewish nation in its Land. The State of Israel is prepared to make its contribution in a concerted effort for the advancement of the entire Middle East.

WE CALL upon the Jewish people throughout the Diaspora to join forces with us in immigration and construction, and to be at our right hand in the great endeavour to fulfil the age-old longing for the redemption of Israel.

WITH TRUST IN THE ROCK OF ISRAEL, we set our hands in witness to this Proclamation, at this session of the Provisional Council of State, on the soil of the homeland, in the city of Tel Aviv, this Sabbath Eve, the fifth day of Iyar, 5708, the fourteenth day of May nineteen forty-eight.

INTRODUCTION

Modern Israel was born a democracy. The decision to establish a Jewish State in accordance with the ruling of the United Nations was taken by the democratically elected leadership of the Zionist Organization, representing Jews the world over, and the Elected Assembly (Asefat ha-Nivḥarim), which represented the *yishuv*, the Jews of Palestine. Both bodies had a long experience of democratic self-rule, with their political parties, representing the popular will, their quasi-parliamentary elected assemblies, and their executives, which were responsible for a wide range of activities usually conducted by governments. Thus it was possible to establish, even before the end of the British Mandate, a National Council and a National Administration, which prepared the ground for statehood and became, on May 15, 1948, as soon as the British had left, the Provisional State Council and Provisional Government of independent Israel. It was characteristic that Israel's leaders were not content with these nominated bodies, but made immediate preparations for democratic elections, which were held on Jan. 25, 1949, before the fighting in the War of Independence had ended.

The dual origin of the provisional institutions was an expression of a central and crucially important feature of the State of Israel. It was not created only by the people living in the country or to serve their interests alone. It was established through the joint efforts of Jews all over the world, through the Zionist Organization and the Jewish Agency, and those who had come to settle in the national homeland as a vanguard for all Jews who should wish to come in the future. Israel, therefore, is not only the home of its present citizens, but the homeland of the Jewish people, open to all Jews who decide to make their homes in it and who, under the Law of Return, 1950, become equal citizens as a matter of right as soon as they set foot on its shores. Others who wish to do so can acquire Israel citizenship after the statutory preliminary period of residence.

While Israel is a Jewish State, Arab and Druze citizens, constituting some 15% of the population, are assured of equality before the law and full democratic rights. They participate in parliamentary and municipal elections, send their representatives to the legislature, and run their own local authorities. The only legal privilege given by law to Jews is the automatic right of entry and citizenship: all citizens, however their citizenship is acquired, are equal, though Arabs are not required, in view of the state of war, to serve in the armed forces.

Israel's democratic institutions are not perfect: they have grown out of the circumstances of its birth and developed under the stress of its tribulations. But they have worked for a quarter of a century and constant efforts are made to improve their working and adapt them to the needs of the times.

Part One:

GOVERNANCE 1880–1948

1 CENTRAL GOVERNMENT

Ottoman Rule: Until the British conquest of Palestine at the end of World War I, the Land of Israel was not a political or administrative unit: officially, there was no such entity as Palestine. The Ottoman Empire was divided into vilayets (provinces), each governed by a Turkish vali dispatched from Constantinople, which were subdivided into sanjaks (districts), each under a mutessarif. Northern Erez Israel formed part of the vilayet of Damascus and, from 1888, of Beirut, while Transjordan belonged to the former. The north of the country comprised the sanjaks of Acre and Nablus, while the south was designated as the independent sanjak of Jerusalem, dependent directly on Constantinople. Sanjaks were further subdivided into *aqdiya* (equivalent to Israel's *nafot,* or sub-districts), each under a *qaimaqam* (equivalent to *kezin ha-nafah,* or district officer). The smallest Turkish subdivision was the *nāḥiya,* containing a number of villages, which was equivalent to the area of the *mo'ezah ezorit* ("rural district") of the State of Israel and was under the jurisdiction of a *mudīr.*

The first Turkish parliament, convened in 1912 in Constantinople, included five delegates from Erez Israel — two each from Jerusalem and Nablus and one from Jaffa. All were Muslims from well-established families. In each vilayet and in the independent sanjak of Jerusalem a *majlis umumi* (popular council) was elected, with one delegate representing every 12,000 male Ottoman taxpayers. Elections were held in Jerusalem only once, in 1910: no Jew was elected, one member was a Christian Arab, and the rest were all Muslim. The councils, which met for 40 days a year under the chairmanship of the vali (or, in Jerusalem, of the mutessarif), had limited advisory powers only. They were, however, suspended altogether at the outbreak of World War I.

In each *qaḍāʾ* of Ereẓ Israel (namely Jerusalem, Jaffa, Hebron, Gaza, Nablus, and Acre) a *majlis idara* (administrative council) also functioned, consisting of the local qadi (Muslim judge); the mufti (Muslim jurisconsult); the heads of the local Jewish, Greek-Orthodox, and Armenian communities; Turkish officials from the local departments of finance and public works and from the *qaimaqam*'s secretariat; and some elected members. In Jerusalem Rabbi Ḥayyim Elyashar was elected.

The country was garrisoned by Turkish troops (one unit was stationed in the Citadel in Jerusalem). Outside the cities a gendarmerie operated, but public security was poor, and blood feuds, sometimes lasting for centuries, were prevalent in the Musiim villages.

British Mandate. From its occupation by British troops in 1917–18 until July 1920. Palestine was under military administration by the so-called Occupied Enemy Territory Administration (OETA "South"—OETA "North" being Lebanon, and OETA "East" Syria and Transjordan). Mandates were given by the Allied and Associated Powers to Great Britain and France to administer these countries (and Iraq) until self-government became practicable. The operation of all these mandates was under supervision by the League of Nations' Permanent Mandates Commission, to which the two powers reported annually on each territory. The Balfour Declaration was embodied in the preamble to the Palestine Mandate.

The administration of Palestine did not differ much from that of a Crown Colony. The governor and (titular) commander in chief was called the high commissioner, who also served as high commissioner for Transjordan with a separate staff in Amman. He was appointed by the Colonial Office and responsible, through it, to the cabinet and Parliament in Britain. During the 28 years of Mandatory government, the incumbents were:

1920–25 Sir Herbert (later Viscount) Samuel
1925–28 Field Marshal Lord Plumer
1928–31 Sir John Chancellor
1931–38 General Sir Arthur Wauchope
1938–44 Sir Harold MacMichael
1944–45 Field Marshal Lord Gort
1945–48 General Sir Alan Cunningham

The high commissioner was advised by an Executive Council, consisting of his principal deputy, the chief secretary (from 1920 to 1922 Sir Wyndham Deedes); the attorney general (from 1920 to 1923 styled legal secretary; until 1931 Norman Bentwich); the treasurer (afterward styled financial secretary); and, from time to time, one or two other members.

In 1920 Herbert Samuel set up a nominated Advisory Council of ten British heads of department ex officiis, four Muslim and three Christian Arabs, and three Jews. After the signature of the peace treaty between Britain and Turkey at Lausanne in June 1922, the Mandate was formally approved by the League of Nations. The Palestine Order in Council (in effect a constitution) came into force on Sept. 1, 1922, and an attempt was made to replace the Palestine nominees on the Advisory Council by elected members—eight Muslim and two Christian Arabs and two Jews. The elections, however, were boycotted by the Arabs on the principal ground that the preamble to the Order in Council incorporated the Balfour Declaration, which they rejected. An Advisory Council consisting exclusively of nominated British officials was therefore set up.

In 1935–6, Arthur Wauchope tried to establish a Legislative Council of twelve elected (eight Muslim Arabs, three Jews, and one Christian Arab) and fifteen nominated members (five British officials, four Jews, three Muslim and two Christian Arabs, and two representatives of commercial interests). The Jews opposed this attempt, since in their opinion it would have endangered the growth of the Jewish National Home. The plan also aroused strong differences among the Arab leaders.

All civil servants were responsible to the chief secretary, save the chief justice (who dealt directly with the high commissioner), and the government auditor (directly responsible to the colonial auditor in London). The officer actually commanding British troops was responsible to the War Office (from 1924 to 1930, to the Air Ministry). The chief secretary's office, known as the Secretariat, dealt with all correspondence between the high commissioner and the Colonial Office and between the chief secretary and heads of departments and district commissioners.

Administrative districts varied in number between seven in 1920 to two in 1925 and to six in 1939; but there were always 18 subdistricts (based on the Ottoman *qaḍā'*). Each district was in the charge of a district commissioner (in place of the former Ottoman *mutessarif*) with a district officer for each subdistrict (in place of the Ottoman *qaimaqam*). The smallest Ottoman unit, the *nāḥiya*, was abolished. All district commissioners were British; at the beginning, so were all district officers, but by the end of the Mandate they were all Palestinians. A new post of assistant district commissioner in charge of one or more subdistricts was created later: at first, all were British; by 1948, several were Palestinian.

In their areas, district commissioners, assistant district commissioners, and district officers represented the Crown. They were primarily responsible for maintaining law and order and coordinating the work of all departmental officers. One of the best-known district commissioners was Ronald Storrs, in Jerusalem. Legislation under the military administration took the form of proclamations, orders, and notices. From 1920 onward, it was by ordinance, approved by the high commissioner in Executive Council, authorized by the Colonial Office, and formally passed without discussion by the wholly British Advisory Council. There also were subordinate regulations, orders and bylaws. All military and civil legislation up to 1934 was codified by R.H. Drayton, a former solicitor general.

6   The Palestine Zionist Executive and, later, the Jewish

Agency were recognized under the Mandate as the competent authority in several matters affecting Jewish development and made frequent representations on questions of major policy. After the enactment of the Religious Communities (Organization) Ordinance in 1926 and of the Jewish Community Regulations the following year, the Va'ad Le'ummi shared with the Agency the responsibility for providing certain services for the *yishuv*, in particular education, health, and social welfare (Va'ad Le'ummi), land development, immigration, settlement, agricultural research, and afforestation (Jewish Agency). Parallel departments—government and Jewish—grew up, facilitating the transfer of authority when Israel became independent.

The Palestine Civil Service in 1948 numbered 10,000, only 250 of whom were British (apart from the British members of the Palestine Police Force, which was not considered part of the civil service). Of the Palestinian civil servants, two-thirds were Arab and one-third Jewish, roughly the demographic ratio. In certain departments (for example, public works), the Jewish proportion was higher; in others (for example, health, curiously enough), it was lower. The proportion of Christian Arabs was much higher than their population ratio and, for lack of suitable education, especially in English, that of Muslim Arabs was much lower.

The budget of the Mandatory Administration rose from under LP2,000,000 (LP1 = £1 sterling) at the beginning to over LP20,000,000 by the end. Even allowing for inflation in World War II, this meant at least a fivefold rise.

2 LOCAL GOVERNMENT

Ottoman Rule. The modernization of local government in the Ottoman Empire began under the vilayet law of
1864, according to which *nāḥiyas,* or rural districts, were
gradually introduced throughout the country. By the end of
Ottoman rule many of the *mudirs,* in charge of *nāḥiyas* and
controlling the villages comprising them, were local Arabs.
Each *nāḥiye* was supposed to have a council, but few were
established. The sheikhs who had exercised authority over
the *ḥamūlas* (village clans) were replaced by mukhtars
(village ḣeadmen), two of whom were to have been elected
in each village together with a council of village elders—the
ikhtiyāriyya. But most mukhtars were appointed rather
than elected, although consideration was given to the
wishes of the local notables. The mukhtar assessed and
levied taxes among the villagers, settled disputes, and
acted as intermediary in the relations between the provincial administration and the village.

The Jewish villages or moshavot, of which there were 28
by the end of the Ottoman rule, were initially outside this
system. They originated their own pattern of self-government, based on Jewish communal self-rule in Eastern
Europe, relying on the self-discipline and loyalty of the
settlers rather than on any legal powers, and resisting
attempts by the Ottoman provincial administration to
control them. The ultimate authority in the moshavah was
the general assembly, which met several times a year. A
village executive committee was elected annually or bian-
nually, and some of the larger moshavot elected village
councils, to which the executive committee was responsible.
The chairman and other officeholders were elected from

among the committee members. In some villages, equal rights were granted, from the start, to all adult members of the community. In others, there were prolonged struggles over political rights between those who owned property in the village and those who did not, mainly the workers. By the end of Ottoman rule, democracy had usually triumphed. Until 1904 the Ottoman provincial authorities paid little attention to the moshavot and their methods of self-government. Then, the four largest were recognized as villages, and those elected by the village council were accepted as mukhtars. By 1914, all moshavot had acquired a similar status.

Municipal government was an innovation of the Ottoman *tanzīmāt* ("reforms"). In 1863 Jerusalem was made a municipality by special imperial firman ("decree"). Under the 1877 Provincial Municipalities Law, 22 towns and larger villages were given municipal status in the 1880s and 1890s. They were provided with an impressive list of duties and legal powers but, in effect, they were under strict surveillance by the provincial district and subdistrict governors. Municipal staffs were pitifully small and incompetent and their budgets minimal. Only Jerusalem had one or two resourceful mayors, who constructed roads and municipal buildings (including a hospital) and introduced street lighting. Tel Aviv was still a suburb of Jaffa. Under the law, municipal councils *(majlis umumī)* of six to twelve members were to be elected by local taxpayers who were Ottoman subjects; in fact, genuine elections rarely took place. In Jerusalem, Jewish and Christian members sat on the council together with Muslim members. Mayors were appointed by the government, usually for short terms of office.

British Mandate. Municipalities. At the beginning of the Mandatory period there were 22 municipalities in western Palestine: 16 Arab and six (Jerusalem, Jaffa, Haifa, Tiberias, Safed, and Hebron) mixed. Tel Aviv, though administered by an autonomous Jewish council, was regarded as a suburb of Jaffa. In 1926 a Municipal

Franchise Ordinance was issued, giving the municipal vote to tenants (males only), even if they held no property, as long as they paid at least one Palestine pound in municipal rates.

A comprehensive Municipal Corporations Ordinance was issued in 1934, authorizing the high commissioner to set up new municipalities or change the boundaries of existing ones on the recommendation of a public committee of inquiry. It prescribed in detail the method of elections, the duties and powers of the councillors and the municipality, sources of revenue (taxes, rates, fees and fines), the procedure for approving the budget, methods of financial control, and the rules for filling major posts, such as those of town clerk, treasurer, town engineer, and medical officer. The procedure for council and committee meetings and the rules for setting up committees were also laid down in detail. The high commissioner retained the right, inherited from the Ottoman rulers, to nominate the mayor and the deputy mayor; bylaws could be passed only on specific subjects listed in the ordinance and subject to the high commissioner's approval. Through the district commissioners, the central government kept the municipalities under strict control.

The ordinance confirmed the unique status of Tel Aviv, which incorporated some older Jewish suburbs of Jaffa and became the world's first all-Jewish city, with the franchise for all residents, men and women—including foreign nationals—who paid as little as LP 0.50 a year in rates. These more democratic provisions were the model for other Jewish councils established later. In Jerusalem, where the Jewish majority had been represented on the municipal council by four members out of 12, there were now six Jewish councillors, four Muslims and two Christians. A Muslim was always appointed by the high commissioner as mayor, however, with a Jew and a Christian as deputies. In 1937 the Jewish deputy was acting mayor for a time, but in the following year another Muslim mayor was appointed.

The first Town Planning Ordinance, issued in 1921, did

not repeal any Ottoman law, but stopped the custom of granting immunity from demolition to an unlawfully built house if the builders had succeeded in covering it with a roof. In 1936 it was replaced by a more modern ordinance, which created local town planning committees identical with the town councils and with the mayor as chairman. These were supervised by the District Town Planning Commissions, headed by the district commissioner, on which government departments were represented, and which received general directives from the central Government Planning Division.

Local and Regional Councils. The Local Council Ordinance of 1921 created a new category of elected local authority. While the Jewish rural communities thought the local council had too little power and authority, the Arab villagers regarded its establishment as interference in their ancient way of life and a threat to the social structure of their communities. During the next five years 21 Arab councils, four Jewish, and one German-Christian (Sarona, near Tel Aviv) were set up. The first Jewish local council established under the ordinance was Petaḥ Tikvah, followed during the next two decades by Rishon le-Zion and Reḥovot (1922), Tel Aviv (1923), Ramat Gan and Afulah (1926), Ḥaderah (1935), Bat Yam, Ra'anannah and Kefar Sava (1936), Bene-Berak and Herzliyyah (1937), and others.

In 1941 the 1921 ordinance was replaced by a new, streamlined one, granting the local councils even more powers than the municipalities and authorizing them to act for the public benefit on any matter so long as they did not come into conflict with other legislation. The high commissioner was empowered, by subsidiary legislation, to declare any village a local council or any group of villages a regional council. Two Jewish rural councils, near Ḥaderah and Petaḥ Tikvah, were set up in 1936–37 to protect the agricultural character of these areas.

By the end of the Mandate, in 1948, 11 small Arab towns and large villages, 26 Jewish villages, and Sarona were local councils, and four groups of Jewish villages were combined to form the Emek Ḥefer, Kishon, Nahalal, and Tel Ḥai regional councils. A new source of income was provided for the local authorities in 1945 by the Local Authorities (Business Tax) Ordinance, which allowed them, after passing a bylaw, to tax businesses operating within their boundaries, subject to approval by the high commissioner.

Villages. In 1944, a Village Administration Ordinance was issued, under which small Arab villages were to elect village councils, with tax powers but under closer supervision by the district commissioner and the central government than the local councils. Up to 1948, 24 were gazetted, in an effort to replace the rule of the elders and mukhtars by democratically elected bodies, but most of them existed only on paper, as the villagers were reluctant to depart from their old ways of life.

Local Government and the Development of the Jewish National Home. The tight control of the Jewish local authorities by the central government often led to tension and was criticized by the Peel Commission in 1937 as hampering advance toward self-rule. The Jewish councils cooperated closely with the national authorities of the *yishuv* and were represented at important meetings of the Asefat ha-Nivḥarim (Elected Assembly) and the Va'ad Le'ummi (National Council), which made continual efforts to enlarge their powers and coordinate their activities. The development of Jewish local government was an important factor in justifying the proposal to set up a Jewish state in part of Palestine and in enabling the *yishuv* to establish independence after the British withdrawal.

3 JEWISH COMMUNAL ORGANIZATION

Throughout this period the Jews of Ereẓ Israel not only had to organize themselves for the purpose of satisfying their religious and cultural needs, but because of the vast difference in culture and standards of living between themselves and the Arab majority, they also had to engage in municipal, political, and economic activities for which the government was nominally responsible. The Ottoman authorities and, from 1918, the British administration performed most of their functions in accordance with the requirements of the Arab majority, while the Turks granted considerable internal freedom to minorities and were usually lax in enforcing law and order. Even before 1918, therefore, the Jewish population assumed some governmental tasks and duties, such as the protection of life and property, the paving of roads and streets, and the administration of justice among its members, while under the British they had, inter alia, to maintain their own educational, social welfare, and health services, apart from those maintained by the government. In addition, the Balfour Declaration and the Mandate conferred upon the Jews certain special rights, not very clearly defined, by virtue of the fact that, although a minority, they were entitled to regard the country as their National Home. This gave an additional impetus to organized Jewish communal life in the land of Israel and endowed the *yishuv* with an importance far transcending its numerical size. The Jewish population also participated, though to a small extent, in some of the general administrative organs. 13

Jewish World Bodies. The communal activities of the *yishuv* were supplemented by the work of world Jewish philanthropic and Zionist organizations, which did not confine themselves to charity, but engaged in agricultural settlement, the maintenance of schools, the provision of health services, and the like. Under the Mandate, in fact, the Zionist Organization and the Jewish Agency undertook a variety of quasi-governmental functions. At the end of the 19th century and the beginning of the 20th, such bodies as the Alliance Israélite Universelle and the Hilfsverein der Deutschen Juden were mainly engaged in educational activity, while Baron Edmond de Rothschild and later the Jewish Colonization Association (ICA) also established agricultural settlements and maintained their communal services. In 1924 the activities of Baron de Rothschild and ICA were taken over by the Palestine Colonization Association (PICA).

The major Zionist bodies active in the country were, during the last two decades of the 19th century, the Russian Ḥibbat Zion movement and, in the first half of the 20th, the World Zionist Organization. Through the Zionist Executive—later the Executive of the enlarged Jewish Agency—it carried out extensive activities in the absorption of immigrants, settlement on the land, and the economic, social, and educational progress of the Jewish population, all of which contributed to the rapid development of Jewish communal life.

The Central Jewish Community. Whatever organized communal life existed in Ereẓ Israel prior to 1900 was confined to local communities. Between 1900 and 1917 three ineffective attempts were made to organize a large part or the whole of the *yishuv*. In 1900 representatives of the Jewish villages in Judea met to further their mutual interests; a year later this organization disintegrated. In 1903 a mission sent from Russia by the Ḥibbat Zion movement, headed by Menahem Ussishkin, convened a *Kenesiyyah* (Congress) of 79 representatives, elected by over 2,000 Jewish dues-paying voters, in Zikhron Ya'akov, with a view to founding a national organization of the *yishuv*. The organization did not outlive the year. In 1913 another attempt to organize also failed.

More fruitful attempts in the same direction were inaugurated at the end of 1917, with the conquest of the country by the British forces, which coincided with the Balfour Declaration. The heterogeneity of the Jewish population and its constantly changing composition were serious difficulties: the formation of a united Jewry proved to be neither easy nor peaceful. There was much opposition and dissension and many obstacles, internal and external, which had to be overcome. The exceedingly diverse social and religious outlooks in the *yishuv* gave rise to a large number of political parties, which also complicated the formation of communal organization.

Between 1917 and 1919 three preparatory assemblies, consisting of delegates from various parties and organizations in the *yishuv*, met to arrange for a Constituent Assembly elected by direct, equal, secret ballot and universal suffrage, including women. The provisional council elected by these assemblies encountered many difficulties. The old *yishuv*, including the ultra-Orthodox and Agudat Israel, were strongly opposed to uniting with nonreligious Jews. The Mizrachi and some sections of the Sephardim objected to giving women the right to vote. Elections to the Constituent Assembly, renamed Asefat ha-Nivḥarim (the Elected Assembly), finally took place in April 1920.

The Asefat ha-Nivḥarim and the Va'ad Le'ummi. Between 1920 and 1948 the Asefat ha-Nivḥarim was the supreme organ of the *yishuv* in conducting its communal affairs. The elections to this body, originally planned to be held every three years or so, were repeatedly postponed because of the exhausting endeavors to reconcile the dissenting views of the numerous parties, the frequent Arab-Jewish disturbances and consequent unrest, and the protracted negotiations with the Mandatory authorities for the legal recognition of the organized Jewish community.

The first two elections to the Asefat ha-Nivḥarim were held prior to the legal recognition of the status of the Jewish community. Though recognition was given in 1928, it took a considerable time to work out the regulations for the election and the various compromises among the parties. The third election was held on a *curia* basis; every voter could vote only in his own *curia*, Ashkenazi, Sephardi, or Yemenite. The number of members for each *curia* was predetermined: 53 Ashkenazi, 15 Sephardi, and three Yemenite. In the fourth election, election by *curiae* was not strictly adhered to.

Jewish Population (composition by curiae; in percentages)

	1918	1928	1943
Ashkenazı	59	71	79.4
Sephardi	33	23	15.9
Yemenite	8	6	4.7

The Asefat ha-Nivḥarim was convened infrequently, for sessions lasting from one to four days, to deal with internal and political issues, organizational matters, and the approval of budgets. The first met three times and the second twice; the third held 18 sessions and the fourth seven. It met for its last working session in October 1947, and the concluding session took place after the establishment of the State of Israel, shortly before the first meeting of the Knesset in February 1949. The Asefat ha-Nivḥarim elected the Va'ad Le'ummi (National Council or, as referred to by the Mandatory authorities, the General Council), which met several times a year and represented the *yishuv* between sessions of the Asefat ha-Nivḥarim. The membership of the Va'ad Le'ummi during 1920–48 varied from 23 to 42, representing almost all parties in the larger body. It elected an Executive of 6 to 14 members, who headed departments of political affairs, local communities, rabbinate, education, health, social welfare, physical culture, and information. The Va'ad Le'ummi was headed by David Yellin (1920–29), Pinḥas Rutenberg (1929–31), Izhak Ben-Zvi (1931–44), and David Remez (1944–48), with Ben-Zvi as president.

The Regulations of the Jewish Community (Knesset Yisrael). In 1930 the first Asefat ha-Nivḥarim decided to prepare a draft constitution for the self-government of the Jewish community and to obtain its formal recognition by the British authorities. It took five years to prepare the document and another three for its legal ratification. The long period of preparation was due to internal differences over the rights of women to vote and the nature of the community: whether it should be based on the personal principle (i.e., as in the Diaspora, for the sole purpose of satisfying religious and cultural needs) or on the territorial principle, according to which the communities should also be vested with all municipal rights and duties. In addition, Agudat Israel did its utmost to prevent the establishment of a united Jewish community not based on strictly Orthodox religious lines, even appealing to the Mandates Commission of the League of Nations.

Negotiations with the British authorities were no easier. The Va'ad Le'ummi, following the conceptions recognized under the Turkish regime, advocated obligatory membership: every person born a Jew was to be considered a member of the community unless he declared himself outside the Jewish ranks. It also wanted the organized Jewish community to have the right to levy compulsory taxes to meet the communal requirements of the *yishuv*. The British were accustomed to the idea of national self-government on a territorial, rather than communal, basis, and wanted the *yishuv* to be a voluntary religious community. Finally, compromises were worked out. In 1926 the Religious Communities Organization Ordinance was promulgated, empowering the authorities to approve for each community regulations which went beyond the satisfaction of its religious needs. Almost two years later, on Jan. 1, 1928, the *Official Gazette* published the Regulations of the 17

Jewish Community, which recognized a Community of the Jews in Palestine, as apart from the local communities. Its central organs were granted judicial powers and the right to levy taxes. Membership was automatic for all Jews after a residence of three months, but once a year any person who wished to have his name struck from the register of the community might do so. The territorial principle was partly recognized in the provision that in any Jewish township, village, or quarter where a local council was established, it could also serve as the local community under the regulations.

The regulations provided for lay authorities—the Asefat ha-Nivḥarim, the Va'ad Le'ummi and the local community—as well as religious ones—the Rabbinical Council and the local rabbinical offices. It took two more years for the parties to agree on election regulations, approved and promulgated early in 1930, under which the elections to the Third Asefat ha-Nivḥarim were held in January 1931. The Regulations of the Jewish Community redefined and confirmed the Rabbinical Council as the supreme religious authority of the *yishuv*. The Council consisted of two chief rabbis, one Ashkenazi and one Sephardi, and six additional rabbis, three Ashkenazi and three Sephardi, all elected by an assembly consisting of 71 members, two-thirds rabbis and one-third lay representatives.

The Local Community. The Jewish local community is older than its countrywide counterpart. The newcomers joined existing Jewish communities in the towns and villages or established new ones in order to satisfy their communal religious, social and cultural needs.

In the towns the local communities were not spared the trials that were the lot of the national organization of the *yishuv*. The same conflicting interests of Sephardi and Ashkenazi congregations, ultra-Orthodox and secularists, property owners and workers, and the numerous parties contributed in varying degrees to the friction that plagued the organized local communities in Jerusalem, Jaffa, Haifa, Tiberias, and Safed. Tel Aviv, established in 1909, gained the status of a local council in 1921 and that of a township in 1922 and, being an all-Jewish community, exercised both communal and municipal functions.

Under Turkish rule and, to a lesser extent, under British administration, the rural Jewish communities, first the moshavot and later the kibbutzim and moshavim, had not only to meet the religious and cultural needs of their members, but also to fulfill municipal functions, such as water supply, sewerage, pavement of roads, protection of life and property, and maintenance of educational, social welfare, and health services. These functions, even when not legally recognized, strengthened the corporate life of the rural community, which was regulated by self-imposed rules and financed by self-imposed taxes.

The Regulations of the Jewish Community provided that only one recognized community might be formed in any one place, but the special religious needs of minorities were considered. The community was granted the right to levy taxes and deal with the communal needs of its members. A system of elections was provided for, and the relations between the community and its local rabbinical office were defined. The supervision of the Va'ad Le'ummi over the local councils was officially exerted, even if not always exercised. Both municipal and communal functions were merged in one authority in the Jewish municipalities and local councils in the country. By 1948 there were two such municipal councils (Tel Aviv and Petaḥ Tikvah) and 26 local councils.

Two generations of intensive communal life, both on the local and the national level, contributed a great deal to the maturity of Jewish public life. On the whole, communal activity became gradually more democratic, and the wide experience in self-government thus gained by the *yishuv* served the State of Israel well in setting up its constitutional organs and administrative machinery.

Part Two:

GOVERNANCE SINCE 1948

1 CENTRAL GOVERNMENT

The establishment by the Declaration of Independence on May 14, 1948, of the Provisional State Council, or legislature, and the Provisional Government of the newly born State of Israel, followed five days later by the enactment of the Law and Administration Ordinance, which specified the powers and procedures of the two bodies, transformed the system of governance from that typical of a colony, with all power vested in the high commissioner, to that of a parliamentary democracy. These provisional institutions consisted mainly of elected members of the executive bodies of the Zionist Organization and the Asefat ha-Nivḥarim of the Jewish community, with heads of a few political groups unrepresented in them. The election by universal suffrage of the Constituent Assembly, which changed its name to "the First Knesset," placed the country's legislative institutions on a firm footing of democratic sanction. In the absence of a constitution the Transition Law (1949), passed by the Knesset at its first session, provided the foundations of the governmental system, regulating the powers of president, parliament, and cabinet and their mutual relationships. Subsequent legislation and amendments, as well as the development of parliamentary practice, elaborated on this basis.

Israel may be designated as a democratic republic with a parliamentary system of government of the strong-cabinet type, a multiparty system with a dominant central party, and a strong tendency toward political and administrative centralization.

The Cabinet. The main policy-determining body is the cabinet, or government *(memshalah)*. All cabinets have been

The Provisional Council of the State of Israel, which served from May 14, 1948 to February 2, 1949. Courtesy Government Press Office Tel Aviv.

based on coalitions of varying political composition, with Mapai (since 1968 the Israel Labor Party) as the major partner. The widest were those of the Provisional Government (in office from independence till March 1949), and the Governments of National Unity in office from the Six-Day War (June 1967) until August 1970. There are few legal provisions regarding the composition of the cabinet. The Basic Law: The Government (1968), which replaces in this respect the Transition Law, provides for a Cabinet composed of the prime minister and an unspecified number of ministers, who may, but do not have to, be members of the Knesset. In practice, most ministers have been Knesset members, though the cabinets of 1965 and 1970 (after the resignation of the Gaḥal ministers) had a third (6 out of 18) who were not. Sometimes, members have resigned their places in the Knesset on appointment as ministers to make way for those next on the list. Ministers may hold one or more portfolios: there may also be ministers without portfolio. A deputy prime minister with unspecified functions, powers, and rank may be appointed: prior to the enactment of the Basic Law: The Government, such appointments were made on three occasions without specific legal warrant.

Partly for reasons of political expediency, i.e., to facilitate the formation of coalitions, cabinets grew from 12 members in 1949 to 24 in 1969, although the number of ministries increased only from 17 to 20. There have been many changes in their composition over the years. In order to safeguard cabinet cohesion and clarify coalition-opposition relationships, collective responsibility and cabinet unity of action, usual in all parliamentary systems, have been reinforced to the extent that a cabinet member may be held responsible for the voting of his party in the Knesset and may be dismissed from office if he or his party do not support the government on a vote.

Cabinet posts are divided among the coalition parties in proportion to their size. In forming governments, the Israel Labor Party has always been guided by two considerations: one, to retain a majority or at least a parity of seats in the cabinet, so as to be able to outvote all the minor partners in unison; the other, to prevent cabinet instability and undue pressure by any single party. The first consideration has worked in the direction of small coalitions; the second has made it necessary to invite at least two smaller parties to join and thus has worked to enlarge cabinets. Ideological considerations have been of secondary importance in coalition formation, but parties regarded as extremist (such 25 as Herut until 1967 and the Communists) were not considered suitable.

The permanence in power of the major government party, the long terms in office of many ministers, and the consistent support of minor coalition partners have helped to bring about a remarkable degree of stability. The fact that 16 governments held office in twenty-four years (1949–73) is somewhat misleading. Only once (in 1951) has a government resigned after a negative vote in the Knesset (and even that was not, strictly speaking, a vote of censure caused by a split among the coalition partners. A few brief cabinet crises, similarly caused by coalition disagreements were followed by the reconstitution of the same government within a period of days. Governments are deemed to have resigned on election day and on the death of the prime minister. They also fall upon the resignation of the prime minister, whether for personal or other reasons.

Coalitions are based on elaborate agreements, which specify in great detail, in addition to the allocation of cabinet posts, the main principles of governmental policy and major items of legislation or administrative action Since national and local elections are, as a rule, held concurrently, the composition of local coalitions has sometimes affected these agreements. For this reason coalition formation has often been a lengthy process having taken on more than one occasion (in 1952–53) over two months.

Complex legal provisions—designed, inter alia, to limit the time spent in the process, now govern the formation of new government. The president, after consultation with representatives of all the parties in the Knesset, entrusts member of Knesset with the task of forming a cabinet. Once he accepts, he has 21 days, which can be extended up to 2 more days, to do so. Should he fail, the president may, but does not have to, appoint someone else to try again, but he has seldom done so, since if the Labor Party nominee could not form a government, no one else could be expected to do so. (In 1950, when Ben-Gurion failed to form a new cabinet

Pinhas Rosen made an unsuccessful attempt to do so and in 1961 Levi Eshkol formed a cabinet headed by Ben-Gurion when the latter felt unable to undertake the task.) In 1951 and 1961, when the Mapai nominee could not manage to get agreement on a new cabinet, the president informed the Knesset, which decided on premature elections. The 1968 law also provides that if the President's nominee cannot form a cabinet, parties constituting a majority in the Knesset may submit a nominee of their own, who must be given the opportunity to undertake the task. In order not to interfere with the essential flow of government business, the law stipulates that any outgoing cabinet continues in office with full powers until a new one is installed. A new cabinet is constituted when it has received a vote of confidence in the Knesset.

Ministers may, with cabinet approval, appoint Knesset members as deputy ministers. They are not cabinet members and their role varies from that of de facto ministers to that of occasional parliamentary spokesman; most have been in charge of a section of their ministry's work under the control of their minister.

The cabinet meets as a rule once a week, on Sundays, to discuss major policy issues and other governmental business and to approve legislation for submission to the Knesset. If necessary, decisions are taken by majority vote and are then covered by collective cabinet responsibility. All cabinet deliberations are officially secret, but in other than security matters it has been found extremely difficult to enforce secrecy. Reports of cabinet proceedings often appear in the daily papers.

Much cabinet business is done by permanent or ad hoc cabinet committees, composed mainly of the ministers directly concerned in proportion to the parties' strength in the cabinet. Committee decisions are final unless challenged full cabinet. The secretary to the government, who informs the press of cabinet decisions, has a small staff to provide clerical services for the cabinet and its committees, prepare the agenda, take minutes, and circulate decisions.

Within the cabinet, the prime minister (*rosh ha-memsha lah*—"head of the government") holds the focal position by being at the center of the policy-making machinery and the seat of political power. This position, although implied by the cabinet system, rests but little on his formal powers; his actual conduct in office enhances this role, which is largely determined by his personality and his conception of the office. Under the Basic Law: The Government, the person who forms the coalition heads it, and as such he has considerable influence over its composition and policy; he has almost full control over the ministers of his own party but much less say, at best a final veto, over those delegated by his coalition partners. On his resignation (or death) the entire cabinet falls, and this provision has been utilized to force an issue with coalition partners or within his own party. Nevertheless, it cannot be claimed that the prime minister is the full and undisputed master of his cabinet. He is very restricted in reshuffling it in connection with any matter of policy without having at least the solid support of his own party.

The most striking innovations in coalition formation and cabinet practice were brought about by the Governments of National Unity after the Six-Day War. The first of these was formally established (June 1967) without even a new cabinet being formed, simply by co-opting three opposition leaders as ministers, and that regardless of the usual coalition formula (i.e., the accepted ratio of one cabinet seat for four seats in the Knesset); the second such government (headed by Golda Meir, March 1969, after Levi Eshkol death in office) was similarly composed. The major innovation, however, pertained to the distinction between two kinds of cabinet membership; one, full membership in the coalition (involving adhesion to the coalition agreements and full collective cabinet responsibility), and the other, accession to National Unity only (in which case only foreign and security affairs, the budget, and vote of censure were covered by the agreement, but the party concerned did not take responsibility for portfolios). The third Government of National Unity formed after the 1969 elections, was constituted on normal lines.

Electoral System. The Basic Law: The Knesset (1958) prescribes that elections must be "universal, nationwide, direct, secret and proportional," and that the electoral system must not be changed unless the amendment is supported by at least 61 out of the 120 members at each stage of the legislative process. All Israel citizens are enfranchised upon completion of their 18th year; candidates for election must be at least 21 years old.

The Knesset is elected by an extreme form of proportional representation, in which the entire country is regarded as one 120-member constituency. Voters have to choose between lists of candidates drawn up by their sponsors—usually party headquarters. Lists may be submitted by parties represented in the Knesset or by new groups: the latter have to be endorsed by a specified number of signatures of supporters and pay a deposit, which is forfeited if the list does not obtain at least 1% of the votes. By a ruling of the High Court of Justice, a list whose candidates can be shown to aim at the destruction of the state may be disqualified: this has only been done on one occasion. To guarantee the utmost fairness, the organization and management of elections are entrusted to a multi-party Central Election Committee, presided over by a Supreme Court justice as impartial chairman. With the various measures safeguarding the secrecy of the vote and providing penalties for pressure of any kind, voting is reasonably free and fair.

Seats are distributed in proportion to the total number of votes obtained by each list. A quota is established by dividing the total votes cast (after deducting spoiled votes and those polled by lists that have failed to get 1% of the total) by the number of seats available (120). In the first place, each list gets one seat for each complete multiple of the quota it polls. At the first elections, in 1949, seats still unallocated after this distribution were allotted by a method resembling the De Hondt system, in force in 29 several European countries, which gave the extra seats to the lists with the largest number of votes per seat. In 195... the system was changed, the unallocated seats going to the lists with the largest remainders. This method wa... regarded as unfair by the large parties, since the size o... the remainder was fortuitous, and in 1973 the previou... system was reinstated, against the fierce opposition of th... smaller parties, by an amendment known as the "Bader Ofer Law" (named after the two members who sponsore... it on behalf of the two largest groupings).

Despite restrictions aimed at curtailing extravagan... electioneering practices, election expenses were at firs... among the highest in the world. The public financing limita... tion, and control of party election expenses was introduce... before the 1969 elections. Each party received the sum c... IL120,000 from the state budget for each of its seats i... the outgoing Knesset and was allowed to spend, from i... own resources, an additional sum of one-third of the treasur... allocation. The election expense accounts were audite... by the State Comptroller. After a successful appeal to th... Supreme Court, the Knesset amended the law to provid... a similar allowance for lists previously unrepresented, bu... according to their seats in the new Knesset. This nove... method of financing actually reduced election expenses ... least by one-half of the previous total. In 1974 a law to f... nance the regular expenditures of political parties, in additio... to their election expenses, was passed. It provided that parti... represented in the outgoing Knesset or the new one shoul... receive a subvention from State funds proportionate t... the number of their members for these purposes, provide... that their books were audited by the State Comptrolle... that they did not spend, in addition, out of their own resourc... more than one-third of the allocation for election expens... and one-half of the allocation for regular expenditure... and that they received contributions to their funds onl... from individuals and not from corporations (paymen... of expenses by the Histadrut to parties participating ... 30 its elections were excepted from the last provision).

percentage of the subvention was withheld until the receipt of a favorable report from the State Comptroller.

The electoral system in force since 1949, more than any other political process, has been the subject of lengthy and at times acrimonious public debates. Its supporters claim it to be the most democratic means of representation, emphasizing national issues and interests and putting a premium on ideological and policy considerations rather than on the merits of individuals and local interests. According to the critics, it makes for dissension and fragmentation, since it enables small groups and factions to achieve representation and political power beyond their actual strength, thereby creating governmental instability and discrediting politics by unsavory bargaining and similar practices. It is a moot point whether the electoral system has actually produced the extreme party fragmentation or is the result of it. In any event, it cannot be gainsaid that proportional representation has perpetuated the situation in which no party has achieved a majority. The Labor-Mapam Alignment, formed in 1968, had at first an overall majority but lost it in the elections in the following year. Proposals to introduce the one-member constituency system were made by Mapai (later the Labor Party), but did not win the support of other parties. In 1972 a Labor-sponsored electoral reform bill under which 90 members would be elected by multi-member constituencies and the rest on a single countrywide list received the statutory minimum of 61 votes on first reading, with the support of the Liberal section of Gaḥal (the Ḥerut-Liberal Bloc) and others, but no further progress was made with the bill before the 1973 elections.

Strict adherence to the purely parliamentary type of government is incompatible with the use of the referendum and similar political processes. Two attempts to hold a plebiscite for the purpose, for example, of changing the electoral law—were defeated.

2 LOCAL GOVERNMENT

In 1949 there were eight municipal councils in the territory of Israel: two Jewish—Tel Aviv and Petaḥ Tikvah; two Arab—Nazareth and Shepharam; and four mixed—Jerusalem, Haifa, Safed, and Tiberias. The councils of Acre, Beersheba, Beth-Shean, Jaffa, Lod (Lydda), Majdal (now part of Ashkelon), and Ramleh had ceased to exist owing to the flight of the Arab inhabitants, and the mixed councils were now wholly or mainly Jewish for the same reason. In Jerusalem, the six Jewish councillors and additional representatives appointed by the Ministry of Interior took over the administration of the New City. There were 24 local councils (one Arab), two Jewish rural councils, and four regional councils.

Like the other laws of the Mandatory regime, British local government legislation was at first automatically taken over, the minister of the interior assuming the powers of the high commissioner, but the Israel legislature took speedy steps to set up a more democratic system of elections and broaden the scope of local self-rule. As hundreds of new villages were set up, new towns founded, and existing ones rapidly expanded, the Ministry of the Interior established additional authorities and helped newly elected representatives to carry out their responsibilities. The first town to be declared a municipality by the Israel government was Netanyah (December 1948). An amendment to the Municipal Corporations Ordinance, enacted at the same time, enfranchised all permanent residents and property owners within the municipal boundaries, fixing 21 (reduced in August 1949 to 18) as the minimum age for voting and 25 (lowered to 20) for election to the council.

In 1950 a comprehensive amendment to the ordinance was passed by the Knesset, providing for fully democratic elections and introducing many new concepts, such as the appointment of an Interior Ministry official as returning officer. The minister relinquished the right to nominate the mayor and his deputy; instead, the councillors elected a mayor and one or more deputies from their own number. The elections were direct and proportional, the voters being called upon to choose between lists of candidates, which were generally submitted by the political parties. A candidate for mayor might have to promise favors or concessions to his colleagues to gain their support, and, as it was rare for any party list to gain an overall majority, coalitions usually had to be formed, with smaller parties often holding the balance. Sometimes agreement depended on the vote of a single councillor, who was tempted to extort advantages for himself and might, on slight provocation, change sides and overthrow the mayor. National party headquarters often gave instructions to their local representatives, and sometimes agreed among themselves that one party would get a particular mayoralty in exchange for another. These complicated maneuvers might even affect the negotiations for government coalitions.

The first municipal elections were held throughout the country on Nov. 12, 1950. In 1953 the Knesset decided that, in future, they should be held simultaneously with the parliamentary polls, thus intensifying political influences on municipal affairs. Election procedure is now governed by the Local Authorities (Elections) Law of 1965, which has been amended five times. It provides, inter alia, that the national voters' register for the area, together with an additional list of all adult permanent residents, including foreign nationals, shall serve as the municipal voters' register. The forty-odd amendments and additions made to the original Municipal Corporations Ordinance between 1948 and 1965 were incorporated in a new, consolidated version, the Municipal Corporations Law, 1965, which has since been amended nine times. In 1973 there were 29 Jew-

A Jerusalem Arab voting in the municipal elections of October, 1969. Photo K. Weiss, Jerusalem.

ish and two Arab municipalities. A bill for the direct election of mayors and heads of local councils was presented to the Knesset in 1969, but was defeated on third reading in 1973. At recent elections, however, voters have tended to support the list headed by the most popular local personality, irrespective of party allegiance.

In the 1973 municipal elections, for example, Teddy Kollek (Labor) in Jerusalem, Shlomo Lahat (Likkud) in Tel Aviv and Yosef Almogi (Labor) in Haifa won more votes than their respective parties in these cities, while in Rishon Le-Zion, Hanania Gibstein (formerly Gahal), standing on an Independent ticket, won 11 out of 15 seats, as against none for the official Likkud list.

Local Councils. The first local council created by the Israel government was that of Metullah, where 84 out of the 101 electors assembled on Nov. 14, 1949, at a general meeting in the community center and elected five councillors. The same procedure, reminiscent of ancient Athenian democracy, was repeated during the following days in Migdal, Rosh-Pinnah, Shavei Zion, and Yesud ha-Ma'alah. Each new council was established by a special, separate order based on the Mandatory Local Councils Ordinance.

In 1950, a combined new order for the larger (class A) local councils was issued, providing for close supervision and control by the district commissioners as the minister's representatives and, in general, adopting the committee system. At the same time a parallel order was issued for smaller (class B) local councils, in response to the needs of the many new villages and small townships founded by recent immigrants, prescribing even greater control by the district commissioner. In view of the rapid growth of these councils in size and number, a new Local Councils Order (class B) was issued in 1953, empowering the minister, if he saw fit, to nominate government officials supplementing the number of councillors by one-third. By October 1969, only 16 Jewish class B councils remained; many had been upgraded to class A, some merged with existing councils, and a few disbanded when their population moved to other localities. Revised and consolidated orders were issued in 1962 and 1963 for for class A and class B councils respectively. In 1965, the Mandatory Local Councils Ordinance of 1941 was republished with all amendments and additions as the Local Councils Law, which has since been amended only once. In 1973 there were 69 Jewish and 47 Arab and Druze local councils.

Regional Councils. In 1949, under the Mandatory Local Councils Ordinance, the minister of the interior issued an order establishing the first regional council, called Emek ha-Yarden, for a group of kibbutzim in the Jordan Valley. The local committee of each kibbutz had to elect at least one of its members to the council. This order served as the model for many more until, in 1958, a revised and consolidated general order was issued. Their are 48 regional councils under the order. They cover over 700 villages—moshavim, kibbutzim, small farms, agricultural schools and institutions. The village committee has to submit its municipal budget every year to the regional council for approval. It may levy rates and pass bylaws, but the privilege has never been used.

Municipal Unions. An original Israel contribution to local government legislation was made in 1955, when Israel Rokach, then minister of the interior, submitted to the Knesset a Municipal Unions Law. He found that many important local projects came to an end at the municipal boundary because there were no legal provisions for cooperation between municipalities. The new law enabled a union to be set up for a specific purpose on the request of a group of local authorities or by order of the minister. The union is run by a council on which the participating local authorities are represented proportionately and whose expenditures are covered by proportional contributions from their budgets. Thirty-two municipal unions have been set up for hospitalization, secondary education, veterinary and agricultural services, slaughterhouses, and other purposes. The first and best known was the Dan Sewerage Union, which, in 1955, undertook to solve one of the major problems of greater Tel Aviv, the disposal of the ever-increasing quantities of sewage water.

Town Planning. The Mandatory Town Planning Ordinance of 1936 was repealed in 1965 by an elaborate

Planning and Building Law, which reverted to the early Mandatory three-tier system: a National Planning Board, District Planning Commissions, and separate local Planning Committees. Under the law the government has to acquire building permits like any private citizen.

Central Supervision. The minister of the interior supervises the activities of the local authorities through six district commissioners and district officers, who operate in 14 subdistricts. If a council's work breaks down through gross inefficiency or chronic dissension among the councillors, the minister may appoint a committee of officials to administer its affairs until the next elections. To supplement the minister's regular, everyday supervision by control of budgets, the ministry has issued the Local Authorities Order (Employment Service), 1962, establishing the Local Authorities Staff Commission as a department of the ministry to control hiring and service of all personnel in local and regional councils. Legislation to impose the authority of the commission on the municipalities has not yet been passed owing to strong opposition on their part.

Under the Law for Drainage and Prevention of Floods, 25 drainage authorities, similar to the municipal unions, have been set up jointly by the ministers of agriculture and the interior to coordinate the work of adjacent local authorities on this area. Other legislation, both Mandatory and Israel, gives local authorities powers and duties in such matters as public health, public entertainment, licensing of trade and industry, the levying of a social-welfare tax, and the maintenance of fire-fighting services.

3 CIVIL SERVICE

The Civil Service of the State of Israel was built up after May 1948 with practically no help from the previous British Mandatory regime, whose senior officials, nearly all British, had left the country. Of the remainder, two thirds had been Arab and some of the Jewish officials did not wish –or were not invited—to continue. With the establishment of the State, the Va'ad Le'ummi was disbanded and its officials were transferred, largely to the newly created ministries of Education, Health, and Social Welfare. Selected officers who had served in the Haganah and in the British forces in World War II took over the Ministry of Defense. Many Jewish Agency officials, belonging to departments whose functions had been taken over by the state, also joined the new civil service. The lower ranks, especially in the postal services and the police, were filled by new immigrants and, increasingly, by sabras.

There is no competitive general civil service entrance examination. The lower grades of the civil service are filled by the labor exchanges. Candidates for appointment to or promotion in the middle and upper grades are chosen by ad hoc selection boards. The point of entry into the civil service depends on the candidate's level of education. Many posts in the middle ranks are reserved for secondary school graduates and, in the upper ranks, for university graduates. Most newly appointed civil servants are given a ministerial induction course. Professional courses, both compulsory and voluntary, are arranged either by ministries or by the Civil Service Commission. Every newly appointed civil servant receives a formal letter of appointment. He must also sign a secrecy pledge.

Table 1. Government Employees, by Ministries, 1972

President's Office	32
Knesset	180
State Comptroller's Office	465
Prime Minister's Office	1,151
Ministry of Finance	7,142
Ministry of Defense	1,965
Ministry of Health	10,125
Interns	53
Ministry of Posts	13,885
Ministry of Religious Affairs	346
Ministry for Foreign Affairs	854
Ministry of Education & Culture	2,508
Ministry of Agriculture	3,337
Ministry of Commerce & Industry	913
Ministry of Police (Office staff)	444
Ministry of Justice	1,438
Ministry of Social Welfare	1,643
Ministry of Labor	3,630
Ministry of Development	181
Ministry of the Interior	736
Ministry of Immigrant Absorption	433
Ministry of Housing	826
Ministry of Transport	
Head Office	1,883
Railroads	2,139
Israel Land Directorate	498
Ministry of Tourism	260
Israel Police Force—Total	*13,534*
Policemen, supernumerary constables	11,958
Prison staff (warders)	1,576
Total Government Employees[1]	**70,749**

[1] Excluding teachers, employees of the State Employment Service and the Broadcasting Authority, and civilian workers in defense establishments.

Table 2. Government Employees, in Standard Grades, 1972

Grade	
A	—
B	—
C	271
D	1,153
E	868
F	1,532
G	2,267
H	3,166
I	3,874
J	4,830
K	5.255
L	4,433
M	2,972
N	2,033
O	1,550
P	1,158
Q	548
R	249
S	114
T	17
Trainees and apprentices	88
Special contract	235
Temporary workers	10,502
TOTAL	**47,115**

There are restrictions on the acceptance of outside employment. Infringements of the disciplinary regulations are dealt with primarily by the ministry concerned; serious offenses are referred to a government disciplinary court, which has power to recommend reprimand, deferment of salary increments, down-grading, or dismissal. Criminal offenses are referred to the police and the courts of law. All civil servants insure themselves with a health insurance fund and are entitled to paid sick leave. In addition to a weekly day of rest and ten days of annual official holidays, each receives from 14 to 26 days of paid annual leave, depending on grade and length of service. Civil servants normally retire at the age of 65. Those holding permanent posts receive pensions based on their length of service. The others receive gratuities. In 1970 there were some 6,600 government pensioners in Israel, some receiving British Mandatory pensions, as well as 3,400 widows and orphans of civil servants.

All civil servants are automatically members of the Civil Servants' Union, which is part of the Histadrut, the General Federation of Labor. Under the terms of a 1949 agreement, the government must obtain the concurrence of the Civil Servants' Union to all basic changes in condition of employment. There are elected staff committees in all ministries and their dependent units. Legislation affecting the service includes: the Civil Service (Pensions) Law, 1955; the Civil Service (Appointments) Law, 1959, providing that all appointments shall be by merit, either through the labor exchanges or, after vacancies have been advertised and applications invited, by properly constituted appointment boards; the Civil Service (Restriction of Political Activity and Fund-raising) Law, 1959; and the Civil Service (Discipline) Law, 1963. Other matters are governed by the Service Regulations (Heb. *Takkanot Sherut*—abbreviated *Takshir*), which are amended from time to time in consultation with the Civil Service Union. Files of the *Takshir*, indexed for easy reference, are issued to all units.

The Civil Service Commission, which in 1970 employed a staff of some 150, is attached to the Ministry of Finance. It is headed by a Civil Service Commissioner with wide powers and the rank of director general. The commission has departments dealing with establishments, salary scales, movement of staff (appointment, promotion, transfer, and termination), conditions of employment, training, and organization and methods. In addition to operating a central school of administration in Jerusalem, the commission provides its own correspondence courses for civil servants in the field and publishes administrative-training textbooks, including Hebrew translations of standard foreign works.

Foreign Service. A blueprint of the Israel Foreign Service had been drawn up even before the establishment of the State of Israel. The first Foreign Minister, Moshe Sharett, had been head of the Jewish Agency's Political Department for 15 years before 1948, and its small staff became the nucleus of the Israel Foreign Service. These men were joined by some of the 25 participants in a course for future public servants, organized by the department in 1946 as the British Mandate drew to its close, and nicknamed "The School for Diplomats."

Until 1953 recruitment was mainly by recommendation; thereafter competitive entrance examinations for cadet diplomats, in which university graduates participated, were introduced. On a few occasions competitive entrance examinations for intermediate ranks of the service have also been held. From time to time, some officers have been appointed on a temporary basis by special contract, or were loaned by other branches of government, public service, or the army. The majority of the heads of mission are career officers. However, the government, upon the recommendation of the foreign minister, occasionally appoints personalities from public life or persons with special qualifications as heads of missions.

In its organizational structure the service is similar to those of other countries, but its members fulfill additional specific tasks. They have to be incessantly on the alert to defend Israel's interests against Arab hostility and cultivate solidarity and cooperation with the Jewish communities in the Diaspora. They must devote particular attention to the Jewish community life, including religious, cultural, and educational activities, particularly activities linked with Israel, such as fund raising, youth movements, immigration, and investment initiatives. Israel diplomacy is also actively engaged in the struggle against all aspects of anti-Jewish discrimination. The trend toward expansion

received a sharp set-back in 1973, when most African countries severed their diplomatic relations with Israel.

The personnel of the service is grouped in three divisions: the political division, the general administrative division, and the home administrative service. Officers of the first two divisions may receive appointments to any part of the world. Political officers may take up either diplomatic or consular posts. There is a general endeavor to observe a roughly uniform system of rotation, whereby officers and their families spend occasional periods of service at home in order to remain in touch with developments in Israel life. To alleviate the difficult problem of a Hebrew education in certain countries, classes with Israel teachers have been organized wherever practicable. Salaries are probably among the lowest in any foreign service in the world.

The quality of the Israel Foreign Service and its ability to implement the foreign policy of the government, to advise wisely on foreign affairs, and to respond effectively to the leadership of the foreign minister are determined primarily by the morale, spirit, knowledge, and capability of its personnel. At the beginning there was mainly an enthusiastic clan of devoted and determined amateurs. Since then the experience of professional diplomacy has been encountered and its methods, generally, mastered. At the same time, however, an unceasing and conscious effort has been made to maintain the traditional values of the Jewish renaissance, a pioneering attitude, and service to Israel. These values, it is considered, must form the essence of the *esprit de corps* of the Israel Foreign Service.

Part Three:

INSTITUTIONS AND INSTRUMENTS OF STATE

1 PRESIDENT

The president of the State of Israel, the official head of state, resembles a constitutional monarch in function and powers, and bears the ancient Hebrew title of *"nasi."* According to the Basic Law: President of the State, passed by the Knesset on June 16, 1964, any citizen of Israel resident in the country is eligible for the office and may hold it for no more than two consecutive terms. The seat of the president is Jerusalem. With the exception of these two provisions, the Basic Law does not differ substantially from the Presidency of the State Law, 1951, which provides that the president must be elected by a majority of all members of the Knesset (i.e., by at least 61 votes) for a five-year term beginning on the day when he makes and signs the declaration of allegiance before the Knesset. He cannot be called to account before any court but he may be deposed by the Knesset for unbecoming behavior or in the case of ill-health, which makes it impossible for him to carry out his duties.

The president signs all laws (other than those concerned with his own powers) and treaties ratified by the Knesset. He appoints (upon the recommendation of the foreign minister) the diplomatic representatives of the state, and accepts the credentials of diplomatic representatives of foreign states accredited to Israel. Upon the recommendation of the appropriate governmental authorities, he appoints the state comptroller, the governor of the Bank of Israel, the members of the civil judiciary, and the judges of the religious courts. The president receives the resignation of the government and sets in motion the process of forming a new government by consultng representatives of

Chaim Weizmann speaking to the Constituent Assembly after having been sworn in as first president of the State of Israel, February 13, 1949. Courtesy Government Press Office, Tel Aviv.

all the political parties in the Knesset and then entrusting a member of the Knesset with the task of setting up a government. He is also given reports of government meetings. The president is empowered to pardon offenders and to mitigate sentences.

The first president of the state, Chaim Weizmann, was elected on Feb. 16, 1949, at the opening session of the First Knesset—held with symbolic significance in Jerusalem, though the seat of the Knesset and government was still in Tel Aviv. He brought to the presidency his extraordinary experience in Zionist leadership and diplomatic negotiation, but illness restricted his activities to the formal duties of the office. Weizmann died on Nov. 9, 1952, and was succeeded by Izhak Ben-Zvi. Under President Ben-Zvi, the official residence and office of the president were established in Jerusalem. There for two full terms and part of a third, until his death on April 23, 1963, Ben-Zvi filled the office with rich human, spiritual, and scholarly content. He and his wife Raḥel made the residence a meeting place for the diverse "tribes of Israel," aiding notably in the process of national amalgamation during those years of mass immigration from Europe and the Islamic countries. The monthly "New Moon" meetings of groups from particular countries and the "Open House" held annually during Sukkot week were typical of the direct contact established with the masses of Israel's citizens, including the Muslim, Druze, Christian, Bahai, and Samaritan communities. President Ben-Zvi paid state visits to Belgium and Holland, to Burma, and to Congo Brazzaville, the Central African Republic, and Liberia.

When Zalman Shazar was elected president on May 21, 1963, he brought with him the qualities of a historian, Israel and Zionist leader, and orator, who had devoted himself to the world Jewish community, its educational problems, and its literature in Hebrew, Yiddish, and other languages. All these interests were expressed in the activities of the president's residence. The Bible Study Circle, originally led by the Prime Minister, David Ben-Gurion, met there regularly, as did the Circle for the Study of the Diaspora under the aegis of the Hebrew University's Institute of Contemporary Jewry. The president instituted a special fund for the encouragement of literature and scholarship and invited outstanding writers, artists, and thinkers from abroad to visit Israel as his guests. He and his wife Raḥel, a writer and women's leader, paid state visits to Nepal, Uruguay, Chile, and Brazil in 1966, and Canada in 1967.

Prof. Ephraim Katzir (Katchalski), who assumed the office of president on May 23, 1973, was a scientist of international renown. Until taking office he had served as head of the Department of Biophysics at the Weizmann Institute of Science; previous roles he had filled include heading the scientific research corps in the Israel Defense Forces.

2 KNESSET

The Knesset (Heb. "Assembly") is the parliament of Israel. It took its name and the number of its members from the *Keneset ha-Gedolah* of the early Second Temple period. It consists of a 120-member single chamber, elected for a four-year term, and is the supreme authority in the state. It elects the president; the government takes office only with its formal approval and must resign if it loses the confidence of the Knesset; its legislative acts are, generally, immune from challenge in the courts.

The Provisional State Council, which exercised legislative authority after the Declaration of Independence, adopted, on Nov. 18, 1948, an ordinance providing for the election of a Constituent Assembly and, although armistice agreements had not yet been signed with Israel's Arab neighbors, the elections were held on Jan. 25, 1949. The electorate numbered 505,567, and 86.8% cast their votes. The Constituent Assembly met for the first time on Feb. 14, 1949, and was opened by Chaim Weizmann, president of the State Council.

Although the Assembly had been expected to adopt a constitution and then disperse for further elections, the majority felt that it should begin immediately to act as a legislature and postpone the adoption of a formal constitution to a later date. On Feb. 16, therefore, the Assembly adopted the Transition Law, laying down, in outline, the constitutional arrangements for the government of the country, the first clause of which stated:

> The legislative body of the State of Israel shall be called the Knesset. The Constituent Assembly shall be called 'the First Knesset.'

On the same day Weizmann was elected president of the state, and the Knesset began to carry out its legislative functions. After prolonged debate, it rejected proposals for the immediate adoption of a comprehensive written constitution, and decided, on June 13, 1950, to enact the chapters of the constitution from time to time in the form of separate laws, to be drafted by its Constitution Committee. Four such "Basic Laws" were passed, dealing with the Knesset (1958), Israel lands (1960), the president (1964), and the government (1968).

The proportional representation system of elections inevitably produces a large number of parties: some twenty lists have been presented at every election, a dozen or so securing seats. No single party secured an overall majority at any of the first six elections, held between 1949 and 1965; all governments were therefore coalitions. The Labor-Mapam Alignment, formed in 1969, however, together with its affiliated Arab lists, won 60 out of the 120 seats, but dropped below this number in 1974.

Only the Knesset can decide to dissolve itself and hold new elections before the end of its normal term. This occurred in 1951 and 1961 when after a cabinet crisis no agreement was reached on the formation of a new government.

Organization. Authority remains with the outgoing Knesset until the new one is formally constituted. The oath to the members of the new Knesset is administered by the oldest member, after which it elects the speaker and his deputies, representing the major parties, who together constitute the presidium. The first speaker was Yosef Sprinzak, who held office until his death in March 1959 and was succeeded by Nahum Nir. The third, Kaddish Luz, was elected in November 1959; the fourth, Reuven Barkatt, in 1969, and the fifth, Israel Yeshayahu, in 1972. There are ten committees, each with 19 members appointed in the same ratio as that of the parties in the Knesset as a whole. They are the Knesset (procedure) Committee and committees on: Constitution, Law, and Justice;

Finance; Economic Affairs; Foreign Affairs and Security; Internal Affairs; Public Services; Education and Culture; Labor; and State Control. Their functions are: to examine, amend, and report on bills referred to them by the Knesset, which are then referred back to the House for final approval; to enquire into the workings of the Executive and other administrative matters and report their findings to the House as a whole. Ministers and, with their permission, senior civil servants, army officers, and ambassadors, may be called to give information. The Knesset normally sits on Monday and Tuesday afternoon and evening and on Wednesday morning. The rest of the time on Mondays, Tuesdays, and Wednesdays and frequently Sundays and Thursdays, is devoted to committee meetings, which occupy more of the members' time than in other parliaments. The plenary sessions of the Knesset do not meet on Sundays and Fridays out of consideration for its Christian and Muslim

Opening session of the seventh Knesset, November 17, 1969. Prime Minister Golda Meir is seen with Foreign Minister Abba Eban on her left, and Minister of the Interior, Ḥayyim Moshe Shapira and Defense Minister Moshe Dayan on her right. Courtesy Government Press Office, Tel Aviv.

members. The Knesset has adopted a number of rules (*takkanot*) to regulate its procedure, which is similar to that of the British House of Commons, but follows some of the features of other parliaments.

The Knesset and the Government. With the assembling of a new Knesset, the government submits its resignation to the president, who, after consulting representatives of the parties, calls on a member of the Knesset to form a new government. After assuring himself of the support of parties together commanding an adequate majority, the prime-minister-elect submits to the House a list of the members of the proposed cabinet, with a detailed statement of its basic principles, and asks for a vote of confidence. The cabinet takes office only on obtaining such a vote, and is automatically held to have resigned if a motion of no-confidence, which may be proposed at any time and takes precedence over all other business, is carried. The same procedure is followed whenever the cabinet resigns. Ministers are normally selected from the members of the Knesset, but non-members may be appointed. Knesset approval, by a vote, is required for the co-option of ministers to the government, but a reallocation of functions among its members need only be reported formally to the House. The latter procedure also applies to the appointment of deputy ministers. Parties not represented in the government coalition are regarded as belonging to the opposition.

The Legislative Process. Formally, the agenda of the Knesset is determined by the speaker together with his deputies; but in practice the government's requirements are generally met, and it has the legislative initiative on major questions.

The following is the progress of a law as it passes through the Knesset: (a) The bill approved by the government is laid on the table of the Knesset, where it rests for at least 48 hours before it is debated. (b) The first reading consists of an explanatory speech by the minister responsible, followed by a debate opened by an opposition member. The length of the debate is fixed by the Knesset committee. (c) The bill is voted upon. It may be "returned to the government" (i.e., defeated) or "sent to committee" (i.e., approved). (d) In the committee stage the bill is discussed in detail by the appropriate committee and amendments moved for adoption or rejection. (e) Those amendments adopted are incorporated in the text of the bill, which is brought back for a second reading to the Knesset plenary by the chairman of the committee or his deputy. Any member whose amendment has been defeated in the committee may resubmit it in plenary session and support it in a short speech. (f) After at least a week's interval, the bill, incorporating all approved amendments, is voted on by the Knesset in third reading. (g) It becomes law after it has been signed by the prime minister, the minister responsible, and the president, and published in *Reshumot* (the Official Gazette; 1948–).

Members and their Prerogatives. Private members may take the initiative in any one of three ways:

(a) Questions. A member may submit a question to a minister, who is obliged to reply from the rostrum of the Knesset within 21 days. After his reply, only one supplementary question is permitted, and that only from the member who asked the original question.

(b) Motions for the agenda. A member may submit a motion asking for a debate on any subject which the government has not included in the agenda. He proposes his motion in a ten-minute speech and the minister concerned replies. Two further motions are permitted—to reject the request for a debate or to refer the matter to a committee for examination and report to the House. Although this procedure leads to no binding decisions, it allows any matter of public importance to be aired.

(c) Private bills. A member may submit a motion asking for leave to introduce a bill on any subject. The bill is introduced by the member in a speech to which a minister usually replies, and the Knesset then votes, without further

debate, on two alternative motions—to reject the bill out of hand or to allow it to go to a committee for preliminary examination. The committee may reject the bill or suggest its revision (this is tantamount to acceptance). One sitting a week is set aside for the consideration of private members' motions and bills. In practice, a member generally seeks the consent of his party before employing one of these devices. The large number of motions and bills submitted by small parties has resulted in a quota system being instituted, based on a party ratio, with a slight advantage to the parties not in the coalition.

Members are protected by an immunity act which absolves them from prosecution for any statement or act performed in the course of their duty and protects them against summary arrest. Proceedings may not be instituted against a member charged with any offense unless the Knesset first withdraws his immunity by a majority vote. Arab and Druze members are provided with a simultaneous translation of the Hebrew speeches into Arabic, while their own speeches, if in Arabic, are followed by a Hebrew translation. Official documents are distributed to them in their own language. *Divrei ha-Keneset* (the "Knesset Record") is published in Hebrew.

The Knesset is a member of the Inter-Parliamentary Union, and a delegation attends its annual conferences.

The Knesset Building. The first Knesset opened in Jerusalem and continued its sittings in Tel Aviv in a converted cinema. In December 1949, when it was decided to transfer the seat of government to Jerusalem, the Knesset was accommodated in a building there originally designed as a bank. A permanent building, erected mainly with a fund bequeathed by James de Rothschild, was opened in August 1966. It was designed by J. Klarwein and Dov Karmi. Like those of many other parliaments, the Knesset building and its environs are protected by a special law, which lays down that within a certain radius from the center of the building the writ of the ordinary police does not run. Within this area, no demonstration or assembly may take place without the speaker's permission, no person can be arrested without his leave, and no person may bear arms unless licensed by him. There is a special guard, commanded by a sergeant at arms, who is directly responsible to the speaker.

3 STATE COMPTROLLER

The office of the State Comptroller was set up in May 1949 under the State Comptroller's Law (5709/1949). Until then, the control office functioned as a continuation of the audit department of the Mandatory government, which dealt only with government departments. In Israel, however, the scope of control was expanded to include secret defense and security branches, local authorities, government, corporations, bodies subsidized in any form by the state (such as institutions of higher learning), and all bodies inspected under any law or Knesset resolution or as requested by the Knesset Finance Committee, or under an agreement with the government. The 1949 law, amended in 1952 and 1958, authorizes the State Comptroller to request, obtain, and examine any material required for his inspection; decide on applying inspection to such bodies as are not automatically subject to it; prescribe guidelines for auditors or corporation accounts; recommend improvements in economy and efficiency; make proposals and publish reports. While he holds certain of the powers of an inquiry committee, the comptroller has no administrative authority to enforce compliance or impose sanctions on inspected bodies. Control is carried out ex post facto (post audit), which implies pre-audit of future similar acts. Inspection embraces all aspects of the activities of bodies under review, save for legislative and judicial acts. Activities and assets are examined from the point of view of legality, efficiency, economy, and probity. A special unit in the Comptroller's Office deals with complaints lodged by the public concerning any institution or matter within his competence. The Comptroller's Office is headed by a director-general and employs some 400 university-trained examiners. There are special advisers on legal, economic, engineering, health, and social welfare matters. Siegfried Moses was the first comptroller, from 1951 to 1961. He was succeeded by Yiẓḥak Nebenzahl. A special Knesset committee was set up in 1973 to consider the State Comptroller's reports.

4 JUDICIARY

Throughout the period from the promulgation of the Ottoman Constitution of 1876 until the present time there have been both secular and religious courts exercising jurisdiction in the territory of the land of Israel, but the extent of the jurisdiction of such courts, the qualifications of the judges thereof and of the persons authorized to plead therein, the procedure thereof and the language of pleading therein have varied from time to time.

UNDER THE OTTOMAN EMPIRE (1876–1917). Under the Ottoman Constitution of 1876 cases under Shari'a (Muslim religious) Courts were given jurisdiction to deal with such matters as property in waqf (Muslim religious trust), inhibitions and the termination of inhibitions, wills, the appointment and removal of guardians and trustees, and the granting of loans from the estates of orphans and waqf estates. They also had jurisdiction to hear suits to decide the shares of heirs to property and suits relating to estates in which letters of administration had to be taken out, as well as all other suits concerning rights under the Shari'a law.

Under the regulations of June 30, 1877, courts were divided into two divisions, namely, civil and criminal, in each of which there were courts of first instance and courts of appeal. In addition, there were Peace Courts and Courts of First Instance presided over by a single judge. Commercial Courts were established in important commercial centers; in other places commercial cases were dealt with by the civil courts. There were three courts of appeal in Palestine, one in each of the sanjaks (districts) of Jerusalem, Balqa (Nablus), and Acre. Finally, there was a Court of Cassation for the whole empire in Constantinople.

UNDER BRITISH ADMINISTRATION, 1917–1948. One of the first acts of the British Military Administration in the Occupied Enemy Territory of Palestine was to reestablish the courts, reopening them in Jerusalem on July 24, 1918. A British army officer, who had been adviser to the Ottoman Ministry of Justice a year before World War I, was the administrative head of all the judges, clerks, and staff of the Civil Courts and laid the foundations of the Palestine judicial system, which was retained with several modifications by the British Civil Administration. The Palestine Order-in-Council, 1922, established Magistrates' Courts, District Courts, the Court of Criminal Assize, and the Supreme Court.

The civil courts were empowered to exercise jurisdiction in all matters and over all persons in Palestine, but they were precluded from exercising jurisdiction in any proceeding whatsoever over the high commissioner or his official or other residence or his official or other property, and no action could be brought against the Government of Palestine or any department thereof unless with the written consent of the high commissioner previously obtained. During the period of the Mandatory regime, nearly all the Ottoman rules of procedure in civil and criminal cases were replaced by rules based upon those obtaining in England save that no provision was made for trial by jury.

Religious Courts. In matters of personal status, namely suits regarding marriage or divorce, alimony, maintenance, guardianship, legitimation and adoption of minors, inhibition from dealing with property of persons who are legally incompetent, successions, wills and legacies, and the administration of the property of absent persons, jurisdiction was conferred by the Palestine Order-in-Council, 1922, upon the courts of the religious communities established and exercising jurisdiction at the date of the Order (Sept. 1, 1922), namely the Muslim Religious Courts, the Rabbinical Courts, and the courts of the nine recognized Christian communities: Eastern (Orthodox), Latin (Catholic), Gregorian Armenian, Armenian (Catholic), Syrian (Catholic),

Chaldean (Uniate), Greek (Catholic) Malkite, Maronite, and Syrian Orthodox. The Muslim Religious Courts were given exclusive jurisdiction in matters of personal status of Muslims and also exclusive jurisdiction in cases of the constitution or internal administration of a waqf constituted for the benefit of Muslims before a Muslim Religious Court, and there was an appeal from the court of the qadi to the Muslim Religious Court of Appeal, whose decision was final. The Rabbinical Courts of the Jewish community and the courts of the several Christian communities had exclusive jurisdiction in matters of marriage and divorce, alimony and confirmation of wills of members of their community, other than foreigners, and jurisdiction in any other matter of personal status of such persons, where all the parties to the action consented to their jurisdiction. The Rabbinical Courts and the courts of the several Christian communities, also had exclusive jurisdiction over any case as to the constitution or internal administration of a waqf or religious endowment constituted before these courts according to the religious law of the community concerned.

The jurisdiction of the Rabbinical Courts and the Christian Religious Courts remained unchanged throughout the period of the Mandatory regime, but that of the Muslim Religious Courts was altered by the Palestine Amendment Order-in-Council, 1939, whereunder they could exercise jurisdiction over Muslims who were foreigners only if, according to their national law, Muslim Religious Courts had jurisdiction over them in matters of personal status. No provision was made in the Palestine Order-in-Council, 1922, for the granting by the courts of orders or decrees in connection with the marriage of persons neither of whom was a Muslim or a member of the Jewish community or of any of the nine recognized Christian communities, or for the dissolution or annulment of such marriages.

In the State of Israel. From 1948. Under section 17 of the Law and Administration Ordinance, 1948, of the Provisional Council of State, the courts existing in the 61 territory of the State of Israel were empowered to continue to function within the scope of the powers conferred upon them by law so long as no new law concerning the courts was enacted.

Jurisdiction of Courts. The Courts Law, 1957, repealed the provisions of the Palestine Order-in-Council, 1922, relating to the Magistrates' Courts, the District Courts, and the Supreme Court and replaced them by provisions which did not differ from them substantially.

Judgments given by a Magistrates' Court are appealable to a District Court, which can also deal with a civil or criminal matter not within the jurisdiction of a Magistrates' Court, a civil counterclaim even if the matter or claim is within the jurisdiction of a Magistrates' Court, any matter not within the exclusive jurisdiction of another court or tribunal, a matter within the concurrent jurisdiction of another court or tribunal so long as it is not dealt with by such other court or tribunal, appeals from judgments and other decisions of a Magistrates' Court, and judgment of Municipal Courts and various administrative tribunals. Judgments of a District Court sitting as a court of first instance are appealable to the Supreme Court. There are five District Courts: in Jerusalem, Tel Aviv-Jaffa, Haifa, Beersheba, and Nazareth. Each has a president, a relieving president, and other judges.

The Supreme Court. The seat of the Supreme Court is in Jerusalem and its area of jurisdiction is the whole area of the state. It has jurisdiction to deal with appeals against judgments and other decisions of the District Courts and when sitting as a High Court of Justice it has jurisdiction to deal with matters in which it deems it necessary to grant relief in the interests of justice and which are not within the jurisdiction of any other court or tribunal. When sitting as a High Court of Justice, it has jurisdiction to order the release of persons unlawfully detained or imprisoned; to order state authorities, local authorities and officials of such authorities, and such other bodies and individuals as exercise any public functions by virtue of law to do or refrain from doing any act in the lawful exercise of their functions or, if they have been unlawfully elected or appointed, to refrain from acting; to order courts, tribunals, and any such bodies and individuals as are vested with

The Supreme Rabbinical Court in session at Hechal Shlomo, Jerusalem. Left to right: Jacob Adess, Ovadia Hadya, and Bezalel Zolti. Courtesy Government Press Office, Tel Aviv.

judicial or quasi-judicial powers by virtue of law, other than Magistrates' Courts, District Courts and Religious Courts, to deal, or to refrain from dealing or from continuing to deal, with a particular matter and to quash any proceeding taken or decision given unlawfully. It may order Religious Courts to deal with a particular matter in accordance with their competence or to refrain from dealing or from continuing to deal with a particular matter otherwise than in accordance with their competence.

Other Courts and Tribunals. There are also Municipal Courts, Tribal Courts, and Military Courts exercising jurisdiction almost identical with that exercised by such courts during the period of the Mandatory regime. There are also some new courts, such as Traffic Magistrates' Courts, Courts Martial, Military Courts established under the Prevention of Infiltration (Offenses and Jurisdiction) Law, 1954, to try offenses under that law, and Labor Courts. Traffic magistrates, appointed in the same way as

A military court trial of two al-Fatḥ terrorists, 1968. One of the accused is giving evidence, with the interpreter on his right. Courtesy Government Press Office, Tel Aviv.

judges of a Magistrates' Court, have jurisdiction to try offenses against the Road Transport Ordinance, or any rules or bylaws made thereunder, while the various Courts Martial and a Courts Martial Appeal Court established under the Military Justice Law, 1955, deal with offenses by soldiers and army employees. Regional Labor Courts and a National Labor Court established as from Sept. 1, 1969, under the Labor Courts Law, 1969, have jurisdiction to deal with claims between employers and workers, disputes between parties to a collective agreement, claims against pension funds, claims between a worker and a workers' organization, and claims under the National Insurance Law (Consolidated Version), 1968; they may also try offenses against certain specified labor laws. An appeal lies from a Regional Labor Court to the National Labor Court.

There are also numerous tribunals, boards, and committees established under various laws to deal with special classes of cases, over many of which a judge presides. Under the Commissions of Enquiry Law, 1968, government appoints a Commission of Enquiry under that law to enquire into, and report upon a matter of vital public importance, and the president of the Supreme Court appoints the chairman, who must be a Supreme Court justice or a district court judge, and other members of the commission. The first committee to be appointed thereunder inquired into the fire at the Al-Aqṣā Mosque in 1969. A notable recent instance is the Agranat Commission, appointed in 1973 to consider questions related to the outbreak and initial stages of the Yom Kippur War.

Religious Courts. Changes in the jurisdiction of the Religious Courts were made by the Israel Legislature, particularly as regards the rabbinical courts, as the Jewish Community Rules were inapplicable in the State of Israel.

Under the Rabbinical Courts Jurisdiction (Marriage and Divorce) Law, 1953, the rabbinical courts have exclusive jurisdiction in matters of marriage and divorce of Jews in Israel, who are nationals or residents of the state, in any matter connected with a suit for divorce between Jews which has been filed therein, whether by the wife or the husband, including maintenance for the wife and for the children of the couple, and claims for *ḥaliẓah* filed therein by a woman against her deceased husband's brother, including maintenance for the woman until the day when *ḥaliẓah* is given. Furthermore, when a Jewish wife sues her Jewish husband or his estate for maintenance in a rabbinical court, otherwise than in connection with divorce, the plea of the defendant that a rabbinical court has no jurisdiction in the matter may not be entertained, and in matters of personal status of Jews in which a Rabbinical Court has not exclusive jurisdiction under the law, it will have jurisdiction after all the parties concerned have expressed their consent thereto.

The Druze Religious Courts Law, 1962, established, for the first time in Israel, a Druze Religious Court and a Druze Religious Court of Appeal. The Druze Religious Court is given exclusive jurisdiction in matters of marriage and divorce of Druze in Israel who are nationals or residents of the state and matters relating to the creation or internal management of a religious trust established before a court under Druze religious law or of a Druze trust established before the coming into force of the Law in accordance with Druze custom otherwise than before a religious or civil court. In matters of personal status of Druze in which a Druze Religious Court has no exclusive jurisdiction under the law, such court will have jurisdiction after all the parties concerned have expressed their consent. The Druze Religious Court of Appeal has jurisdiction to deal with appeals from judgments of the Druze Religious Courts.

Matters of dissolution of marriage, including divorce, annulment of marriage, and recognition of a marriage as void *ab initio,* which are not within the exclusive jurisdiction of a Jewish, Muslim, Christian, or Druze Religious Court, are within the jurisdiction of the District Court or a Religious Court as determined by the president of the Supreme Court in accordance with the provisions of the Jurisdiction in Matters of Dissolution of Marriage (Special

Cases) Law, 1969. That law will not apply if both spouses are Jews, Muslims, Druze or members of one of the Christian communities with a Religious Court in Israel.

Appointments and Qualifications of Judges, etc. Under the Judges Law, 1953, an entirely new system of appointment was created: all the judges of the Magistrates' Courts, the District Courts and the Supreme Court are appointed by the president of the state upon the recommendation of a Nominations Committee submitted to him by the minister of justice, who is its chairman. The Nominations Committee is composed of three judges, namely, the president of the Supreme Court and two other judges of the Supreme Court elected by the judges of that court for three years; two members of the government, namely the minister of justice and one other member chosen by the government; two members of the Knesset elected by it by secret ballot; and two practicing advocates elected by the Chamber of Advocates. Candidates for appointment may be proposed by the minister of justice, the president of the Supreme Court, or jointly by three members of the nominations committee.

Similar systems of appointment have been created for judges of the Rabbinical Courts, the Muslim Religious Courts, and the Druze Religious Courts, but no legislation has yet been passed regulating the appointment of the judges of the Christian Religious Courts, who continue to be appointed by the head of the community. Under the Dayyanim Law, 1955, the judges of the Rabbinical Courts, known as *dayyanim* are appointed by the president of the state upon the recommendation of a Nominations Committee submitted to him by the minister for religious affairs. The committee is composed of the two chief rabbis of Israel, two *dayyanim* elected by the body of *dayyanim* for three years, two members of the government, namely, the minister for religious affairs and one other member chosen by the government, two members of the Knesset elected by it by secret ballot, and two practicing advocates elected by the Chamber of Advocates.

Under the Qadis Law, 1961, the judges of the Muslim Religious Courts, known as qadis, are appointed by the president of the state upon the recommendation of a Nominations Committee submitted to him by the minister for religious affairs. The Nominations Committee is composed of two qadis elected by the body of qadis for three years, two members of the government, namely, the minister for religious affairs and one other member chosen by the government, three members of the Knesset, including at least two Muslims, elected by the Knesset by secret ballot, and two advocates, including at least one Muslim, appointed by the Chamber of Advocates.

Under the Druze Religious Courts Law, 1962, judges of the Druze Religious Courts, known as qadis *madhhab*, are appointed by the president of the state upon the recommendation of a Nominations Committee submitted to him by the minister for religious affairs. The Nominations Committee is composed of the chairman of the Druze Religious Council constituted by rules made by the minister for religious affairs under the Religious Communities (Organization) Ordinance, the president of the Druze Religious Court of Appeal, or, if he serves also as the chairman of the Druze Religious Council, a qadi *madhhab* elected by the body of qadis *madhhab* for three years, another qadi *madhhab* similarly elected, the minister for religious affairs and the minister of justice, two Druze members of the Knesset (or other Druze, if there is only one Druze member of the Knesset or none) elected by the Knesset by secret ballot and an advocate elected by the National Council of the Chamber of Advocates for three years.

Every person appointed as a judge, *dayyan*, qadi, or qadi *madhhab* must, before assuming his office, make before the president of the state a declaration whereby he pledges himself to bear allegiance to the State of Israel, to dispense justice fairly, not to pervert the law and to show no favor, while every judge must also pledge himself to bear allegiance to the laws of the State of Israel. Every judge, qadi, and qadi *madhhab* in judicial matters is expressly declared by the law applicable to him to be subject to no authority other than that of the law, while under the Dayyanim Law, 1955, every *dayyan* in judicial matters is expressly to be subject to no authority other than that of the law according to which he judges. The reason for the difference in wording as regards the *dayyanim* is to make it clear that only the laws concerning the legal system of the *dayyanim*, including those laws which restrict the jurisdiction of the *dayyanim* and no other laws, bind the *dayyanim* in judicial matters. Every judge, *dayyan*, qadi, and qadi *madhhab* will hold office from the day of his declaration of allegiance and his tenure will end only upon his death, resignation, retirement on pension, or removal from office by virtue of the law applicable to him.

The qadi, Sheikh Hasan Emir al-Ḥabash, officiating in the Muslim Shariʿa Court at Ṭayyiba, 1962. Courtesy Government Press Office, Tel Aviv.

Every judge, *dayyan,* qadi and qadi *madhhab* is subject to the jurisdiction of a Court of Discipline constituted under the law applicable to him. The Court of Discipline for judges consists of five members, including three judges of the Supreme Court, as the president of the Supreme Court may in respect of each case prescribe, and its members are appointed in respect of each case by the body of the judges of the Supreme Court. Similar provisions apply, *mutatis mutandis,* to *dayyanim,* qadis and qadis *madhhab.*

The salaries and other payments to be made to a judge, *dayyan,* qadi and qadi *madhhab* during and after his period of tenure, including those to be made to his dependents after his death, are fixed by resolution of the Knesset or by the Finance Committee of the Knesset if so authorized by the Knesset.

The Bar. The members of the Law Council were appointed by the minister of justice until a self-governing integrated bar was set up under the Chamber of Advocates Law, 1961. Under that law advocates are subject to the jurisdiction of Disciplinary Tribunals composed solely of advocates as prescribed by the Chamber of Advocates Law, 1961. From a judgment of a Disciplinary Tribunal both the accused advocate and the attorney general may appeal to the National Disciplinary Tribunal and an accused advocate may appeal from a conviction by the National Disciplinary Tribunal to the Supreme Court. There are about 4,000 members of the Chamber of Advocates, of whom 200 are in public service.

5 LEGISLATION

UNDER THE OTTOMAN EMPIRE. Under the laws of the Ottoman Constitution of 1876 the sultan was empowered to sanction and promulgate all legislation, to make proposals for all kinds of laws, and to safeguard and enforce the rules of the Shari'a and the laws of the state. Islam was the religion of the Ottoman Empire, but subject thereto the state was required to protect the free exercise of all religions recognized in the empire and the integral enjoyment, in accordance with previous practice, of all religious privileges granted to the various communities, provided that such religions were not contrary to public morals or conducive to the disturbance of public order. All Ottoman subjects were equal in the eyes of the law as regards both rights and duties, except for matters relating to religion. Turkish was the official language of the state.

The Ottoman laws were of three categories: those written originally in Turkish, those written originally in Arabic and translated into Turkish, and those written originally in a European language, mainly French, and translated into Turkish. The most important of those laws written originally in Arabic is the Mejelle, an elaborate code of 1,851 articles containing rules of law and maxims of Muhammadan jurisprudence. It is little more than a Turkish translation from the Arab authorities on Muhammadan law, which is based primarily on the Koran and custom.

French influence reigned supreme in the Ottoman Empire from the early part of the 19th century, when the Turkish sultans, who were the sole legislators, began to carry out the legal reforms insisted upon by the European powers. To save time and trouble they borrowed almost en bloc the principal legal codes of France, such as the commercial, maritime, civil procedure, and criminal codes. This borrowing process continued almost without interruption until Turkey entered World War I. It is therefore impossible fully to understand Ottoman legal principles without a study of French law, and Turkish lawyers and judges frequently consulted French legal textbooks and court decisions on difficult or disputed points of law.

UNDER THE MANDATE. Under the Mandate for Palestine, confirmed by the Council of the League of Nations on July 24, 1922, His Britannic Majesty, who had been selected by the principal Allied Powers as mandatory for Palestine, was given full powers of legislation and of administration in Palestine save as such powers were limited by the terms of the Mandate. Under article 15, the mandatory was required to ensure complete freedom of conscience and the free exercise of all forms of worship for all, subject only to the maintenance of public order and morals. There was to be no discrimination of any kind between the inhabitants of Palestine on grounds of race, religion, or language, and no one was to be excluded from the country on the sole ground of his religious belief.

The Palestine Order-in-Council, 1922, was made by His Britannic Majesty by virtue and in exercise of his powers in that behalf by the U. K. Foreign Jurisdiction Act, 1890 or otherwise, and came into force on Sept. 1, 1922. It provided (article 46) that the jurisdiction of the civil courts should be exercised in conformity with the Ottoman law in force in Palestine on Nov. 1, 1914 (the date when Turkey entered World War I), such later Ottoman laws as had been or might be declared to be in force by public notice, and such orders-in-council, ordinances, and regulations as were in force in Palestine at the date of the commencement of the order (Sept. 1, 1922) or might thereafter be applied or enacted. Subject thereto, and so far as the same should not extend or apply, the jurisdiction of the courts should be exercised in conformity with the substance of the common aw and the doctrines of equity in force in England, so far as he circumstances of Palestine and its inhabitants and the imits of His Majesty's jurisdiction permitted and subject to such qualification as local circumstances rendered necessary.

By article 3 of the Palestine (Amendment) Order-in-Council, 1923, the power to legislate in and for Palestine was vested in the high commissioner appointed by His Majesty in council, and it was exercised by him alone throughout the period of the mandatory regime.

Every ordinance promulgated by the high commissioner was subject to disallowance by His Majesty within one year of the date of its promulgation, while certain classes of ordinance could not be promulgated by the high commissioner unless he had previously obtained instructions thereupon from one of His Majesty's principal secretaries of state.

For the most part, by the time the Mandate was terminated, Palestine legislation had replaced the Ottoman law which formed part of the law of Palestine on Nov. 1, 1914, when Turkey entered the war, although some important parts of it, including part of the civil law (Mejelle) and the Land Law, were not replaced.

IN THE STATE OF ISRAEL. The Declaration of Independence, issued by the National Council (Mo'eẓet ha-Am) on May 14, 1948, repealed the provisions of law emanating from the British White Paper of 1939—in particular, the severe restrictions on immigration and on land-transfers to Jews. It declared that the laws existing in Palestine on May 14, 1948, should be in force in Israel insofar as would be consistent with the provisions of the proclamation, with any future laws passed by or with the authority of the Provisional Council of State, and with the modifications emanating from the establishment of the state and its authorities.

The first law to be enacted by the Provisional Council of State was the Law and Administration Ordinance, 1948, passed on May 19, with retroactive effect from May 14,

1948. It provided that the Provisional Council of State was the legislative authority and its executive arm, the National Administration (Minhelet ha-Am) was the provisional government. Laws, which were to be called "ordinances" (the designation used under Mandatory rule), were to be signed by the prime minister, the minister of justice, and the minister or ministers charged with their implementation.

During the nine months of its existence (May 14, 1948–Feb. 14, 1949), the Provisional Council of State enacted 98 ordinances and the various ministers made 34 sets of emergency regulations. Generally speaking, the provisions of the emergency regulations were subsequently incorporated, with certain modifications, in ordinances enacted by the Provisional Council of State. On Nov. 18, 1948, ten days after a census of the population was taken, the Provisional Council of State passed an ordinance providing for the holding of elections to the Constituent Assembly of 120 members. On Feb. 14, 1949, the Constituent Assembly held its inaugural meeting, and two days later it passed its first law, the Transition Law, 1949, which provided that the legislature of Israel was to be known as the "Knesset," and the Constituent Assembly as the "First Knesset," and that the legislative acts of the Israel legislature should henceforth be known as "laws."

There are no restrictions upon the legislative powers of the Knesset, for no written constitution has been adopted. For this reason no Israel court can declare a law of the Knesset unconstitutional as regards its contents, although in 1970 the Supreme Court ruled that a law dealing with the defraying of election expenses had not been passed by the special majority required by the Basic Law: the Knesset (see Central Government, above). During the term of the First Knesset there were long and recurrent debates, both within the Knesset and among the general public in Israel, on the question of whether or not there should be a written constitution. Those debates were ended by the following compromise resolution passed by the First Knesset on June 13, 1950: "The Knesset resolves to impose upon the

Constitution, Law and Justice Committee the task of preparing a draft constitution for the state. The constitution will be built up chapter by chapter in such manner that each chapter will constitute a fundamental law in itself. The chapters will be brought before the Knesset as the committee completes its work, and all the chapters together will be incorporated in the Constitution of the State." So far the Knesset has enacted four basic laws dealing with the Knesset, Israel lands, the president of the state, and the government respectively.

Israel laws are written in Hebrew, and official translations in Arabic and English, prepared in the Ministry of Justice, are published. Under the Interpretation Ordinance, where there is any discrepancy between the Hebrew text and the official translation, the Hebrew text prevails. Where there is any discrepancy between the English text and any other text of any enactment passed before the establishment of the state and not published in a new Hebrew version under section 16 of the Law and Administration Ordinance, 1948, the English text prevails.

The vast majority of the laws passed by the Israel legislature have their counterparts in the legislation of most other countries, but some of them are peculiar to Israel, owing to its being a Jewish state and the realization of the aims of Zionism. Among these are: the Law of Return, 1950, under which the right of every Jew to settle in Israel is recognized, and the World Zionist Organization—Jewish Agency (Status) Law, 1952, which regulates the status of the World Zionist Organization in Israel and its relationship to the state. Laws relating to Jewish law and religion cover such subjects as *kasher* food for soldiers (1948), Jewish religious services budgets (1949), the Chief Rabbinate Council (1955), the jurisdiction of religious courts in marriage and divorce (1953), *dayyanim* (1955), and the prohibition of pig breeding (1962). Furthermore, whenever legislation is required on any particular subject, the relevant principles of Jewish law, if any, are examined and, if found suitable, 75 incorporated. Original Israel laws relating to non-Jewish communities deal with qadis (Muslim religious judges) and the composition and authority of Druze religious courts. On June 27, 1967, less than two weeks after the Six-Day War, the Knesset passed a law for the protection of all holy places under Israel jurisdiction. The Holocaust and its consequences have led to the enactment of laws on the punishment of Nazis and their collaborators (1950), the establishment and administration of the Yad Vashem Memorial Authority (1953), compensation for those disabled in the war against the Nazis (1954) or by Nazi persecution (1957), and Holocaust Memorial Day (1959).

Altogether over 1,400 ordinances and laws have been passed by the Israel legislature, but nevertheless much has still to be done to replace the heterogeneous body of Israel law, originally written in Turkish, Arabic, French, English, and Hebrew, by a homogeneous body of law written only in Hebrew and suited to the needs of the modern, progressive State of Israel.

6 POLICE

The effective establishment of the Israel Police preceded that of the State itself. At the end of 1947, after the United Nations partition decision, the Mandatory police began to break up. Non-Jewish constables were withdrawn from the coastal area; only about 700 Jewish policemen and a little inferior equipment were left. The most serious problem was the shortage of men to fill command and technical posts, most of which had been held by British officers. Second in urgency was the need to change the character of the Police, which, especially in the few preceding years, had been more military than constabulary, into the kind of force normal in a democracy, dedicated only to ensure the rule of law and the public welfare. At the end of 1948, the Police had a strength of 1,882.

Three stages of development may be distinguished. The first was organization and recruitment. This was not easy, for the army demanded first choice of men and material. Nevertheless, within two years 3,497 men had joined, and equipment was assembled from whatever source, regardless of uniformity. In organization and methods, new forms had to be found to fit new needs. Mass *aliyah*, unemployment, and a flood of new legislation naturally enlarged the scope of police work. Relations between the people and the Police were not good, partly because of the aftereffects of the Holocaust and of two wars, and the suspicions of newcomers from eastern European and Arab lands where the policeman was suspect and disliked. Policemen often found themselves confronted by angry demonstrators in front of Government or public offices; the men were pressed into service day and night, with inadequate compensation. The

Policeman on duty in Jerusalem. Courtesy Ministry for Foreign Affairs, Jerusalem.

growing manpower, with a large turnover, was also troublesome. In the second stage, fall-out was heavy, but these were years of natural selection, which strengthened those who stayed on, contributed to their professional specialization and built up a cadre of experts and officers. By the second half of the 1950s long-range planning was
78 feasible and different techniques could be tried out in

organization and command, in criminal investigation and traffic control. Some of these were borrowed, but most were the fruit of the force's own ideas and experience. This was a period of ever-increasing traffic and accidents, security problems complicated by border infiltration, and more crime. In the third stage administration and organization were stabilized and efficiency was steadily increased.

A task unknown to most other police forces is the guarding of the cease-fire lines against infiltration and attack from the neighboring countries. This is done by the Frontier Guard, in cooperation with the army. Some of the girls entering the army are now seconded to the police to help in maintaining vigilance in the three main cities. After the Six-Day War, the Israel Police was also responsible for law and order in the areas administered under the cease-fire agreements. Local Arab policemen, 90% of whom served under Jordanian and Egyptian rule, were recruited and retrained for the purpose. The Israel Police is controlled by national headquarters in Jerusalem and commanded by the Inspector General. There are three districts, Northern, Tel Aviv and Southern, with headquarters in Nazareth, Tel Aviv and Jerusalem respectively, which are divided into sub-districts, stations, and posts. The transfer of national headquarters from Tel Aviv to Jerusalem started in 1969. The strength of the force in 1972 was 12,850, including 1,200 Israel Arabs and Druze, and about 1,000 local personnel in the administered areas. Some 1,200 were women.

POLICE RANKS

Melakke'aḥ Kelali	Inspector General
Niẓẓav	Commander
Niẓẓav-Mishneh	Deputy Commander
Segan-Niẓẓav	Chief Superintendent
Rav-Pakad	Superintendent
Pakad	Chief Inspector
Mefakke'aḥ	Inspector
Segan-Mefakke'aḥ	Assistant Inspector

7 ISRAEL DEFENSE FORCES

Israel Defense Forces (abbr. IDF: Heb. צְבָא הֲגַנָּה לְיִשְׂרָאֵל :
Zeva Haganah le-Israel; abbr. צה״ל , *Zahal*) was
established on May 26, 1948, by the provisional government of the State of Israel, and on May 31, 1948,
the first official oath-taking ceremony took place. It is
unique in the armies of the world in the degree to which it
has succeeded in eliminating distance between itself and the
people that it serves; indeed it is an organic part of the
people. This closeness results from the fact that the IDF is
essentially based on reserve service of the civilian population. Accordingly, and primarily due to this reason, it has
not developed into a standard professional army but has
retained more of the pre-state character of a popular
militia. Because of its popular character and the fact that
the youth of the country, without exception, have to pass
through its ranks, the IDF has proved to be one of the most
important factors in effecting the integration of the various
cultural elements of the population of Israel. In the early
days of the state, the IDF probably had more influence in
this respect than any other single element, and today it is on
a par with the school system in bringing about national
integration. It has taken an active part in the educational
integration of the new immigrants in the country by
conducting intensive courses to raise all ranks to a
minimum educational standard and by allocating women
teachers to immigrant villages with a view to raising the
standard of education there. The army continues to supply
these services as well as providing additional facilities for
more advanced education of its officers and men up to and
including university education. In times of national stress

(not only military) the IDF has been in the forefront. The great waves of immigration in the early 1950s, which posed major organizational problems, were successfully absorbed with the help of the army, which also assisted in conducting welfare activities in the immigrant camps.

TERMS OF SERVICE. From its inception, Israel established a system of compulsory military service that requires both men and women of certain ages to report for varying periods. Men aged 18–55 (inclusive) and women aged 18–38 (inclusive)—Israel citizens and permanent residents of the country—are liable for service. The law governing military service is the Security Service Law, 1959. The IDF comprises three types of service: conscript service, reserve service, and regular service. Men aged 18–29 (inclusive), women aged 18–26 (inclusive), and licensed medical practitioners aged 18–38 (inclusive both men and women) are liable for conscript service. From the late 1960s, the period of service for conscript males aged 18–26 is 36 months and for males aged 27–29 is 24 months; new immigrants aged 27–29 serve 18 months. The period of service for women is 24 months, although, in fact, they now serve only 20 months. The minister of defense is authorized to recognize service in the Border Police as military service within the framework of the law.

On conclusion of his conscript service, every soldier is assigned to a reserve unit. Within the framework of the law, a reservist may be called for service one day per month or alternatively three days per three months. The law sets out maximum periods of service as follows: men in the rank of private *(turai)* and lance corporal *(turai rishon)* aged 18–39 (inclusive) serve 31 days per annum, and those aged 40–54, 14 days per annum. Corporals *(rav turai)* and above may be asked to serve an additional seven days to the above periods. Privates and lance-corporals of the women's forces are liable for 31 days per annum and corporals and above for an additional seven days service per annum. Men aged 45–54 are liable for service only in the Civil Defense organization, unless their rank is that of second lieutenant

Tura'i	Private
Tura'i Rishon	Lance Corporal
Rav Tura'i	Corporal
Sammal	Sergeant
Sammal Rishon	First Sergeant
Rav Sammal	Sergeant Major

Officer Ranks

Segen Mishneh	Second Lieutenant
Segen	Lieutenant
Seren	Captain
Rav Seren	Major
Segan Aluf	Lieutenant Colonel
Aluf Mishneh	Colonel
Tat Aluf	Brigadier General
Aluf	Major General
Rav Aluf *	Lieutenant General

* The rank of *Rav Aluf* is held only by the Chief of Staff of the Armed Forces.

(segen mishneh) and above or the reservist's specialization is a required one, as determined by the minister of defence in accordance with the regulations of the law.

In addition to the monthly and annual reserve service, every reservist is liable for what is known as "Special Service." The minister of defense may, if he is satisfied that the defense of the state so requires, mobilize any reservist for conscript or reserve service in such locations and for such periods as his order specifies. This order can be a general one or can refer to specific units or specific persons. In the event that such an order is issued, the minister of defense is required to bring it to the knowledge of the Knesset Foreign Affairs and Defense Committee as soon as possible. The committee may or may not approve the order with or without changes, or may bring it before the Knesset. It lapses within 14 days if not approved by the Foreign Affairs and Defense Committee or by the Knesset before the conclusion of the stated period. Such an order, was issued, for example, at the time of the Yom Kippur War in 1973, when reserves were mobilized for an extended period.

Mothers and pregnant women are exempt from national service within the framework of the Security Service Law. Married women are exempt from conscript service but not from reserve service. The law provides for the exemption of women from service on the basis of religious reasons.

Composition of the IDF. The IDF is composed of three elements: regular officers and N.C.O.s; the standing army, which is composed of the regular officers, N.C.O.s and conscripts; and reserve forces, which are mobilized at any given time. Officers and N.C.O.s may volunteer for regular service in the armed forces after they have completed their conscript service. They can commit themselves for varying periods ranging from one to five years. Their conditions of service, rates of pay, and so on are linked to those prevailing in the government civil service. The mandatory age of retirement is 55, but regulars who have completed a minimum of ten years' service and have reached the age of 40 may be authorized by the chief of staff to retire on partial pension, based on the payment of 2% per annum of service and related to their last rank.

Organization of the Forces. The IDF is subject to the orders of the government of Israel and carries out its policy. The minister of defense is responsible to the government and issues the instructions of the civilian authority to the armed forces. A special ministerial defense committee deals in detail with defense problems on behalf of the Cabinet. Military matters in the Knesset are dealt with, usually in closed session, by the Foreign Affairs and Defense Committee, which also deals, jointly with the Finance Committee, with budgetary matters related to the armed forces. The Ministry of Defense includes the minister of defense's personal staff and is divided into departments dealing with the following subjects: procurement of weapons and equipment; research and development; military industries; the aircraft industries; and manpower problems, such as rehabilitation, disabled ex-servicemen, responsibility for service widows and orphans, and military cemeteries; building and properties; sales; data-processing units; foreign aid; youth and Naḥal division; Gadna division; public relations; *shekem* ("canteen services"); soldiers' welfare committee; legal advice; and financial control. The senior military authority is the chief of staff, who commands all the armed forces. The chief of staff is nominated by the minister of defense and appointed by the government. The period of service of the chief of staff is usually three to four years.

The IDF is an integrated organization controlling the land, sea, and air forces. Operationally, the armed forces are divided into three regional ground commands, Northern, Central, and Southern, in addition to the air force and the navy. The commanders of the air force and the navy are at the same time senior advisers to the chief of staff in their respective functions. The chief of staff heads the General Staff, which functions in the general headquarters of the IDF. This organization is responsible for carrying out the security policy of the State of Israel and for controlling the IDF in times of war and peace. On occasion there has been a vice-chief of staff. Failing such an appointment, the chief of the General Staff Branch replaces the chief of staff in his absence.

The General Staff is divided into five branches, each headed by a major general. The General Staff Branch is responsible for the operational control of the armed forces, including training, organization and operations. The Planning Branch is responsible for research and development. The Intelligence Branch is responsible for the collection, collation, and dissemination of all military, political, and economic information that might be of interest to the General Staff for the purpose of planning and of operations, as well as the security within the armed forces, censorship, the official army spokesman, liaison with foreign attachés, and the appointment of Israel military attachés abroad. The Manpower

Branch is responsible for the mobilization of the manpower required by the IDF, for the assignment of men to units, for planning and control of manpower, education, personal services, discipline, information, religious and medical services, etc. The Quartermaster General Branch is responsible for the organization of the supply of equipment, arms, food, clothing, housing, etc., for the maintenance of emergency stores, and for the readiness of all administrative emergency organizations falling within its area of responsibility.

In addition to the regional commands and the air force and navy, the commanders of which hold the rank of major general and control all the forces within their particular command, there are a number of specific commands.

The Training Command sets the training objectives of the General Staff and controls and operates all the military schools and training bases within the IDF.

The Armored Command is directly under the command of the General Staff. It is entrusted with the task of developing the armored strength of the IDF and its doctrine, training programs, and equipment.

Naḥal is a special organization, unique to the IDF. Its initials stand for No'ar Ḥaluẓi Loḥem ("Fighting Pioneer Youth"). New settlement has always been considered important in Ereẓ Israel from a security point of view, especially in the border areas. With this consideration in mind, a special corps was established that combines military and agricultural training and also engages in the establishment of new settlements along the borders. Upon conclusion of military service, those Naḥal soldiers who wish to return to civilian life do so, while others remain and continue to live in the kibbutz. As long as a new settlement is not self-supporting, it remains within Naḥal, under military discipline and tied organically to the army. When the settlement has developed and begins to be self-supporting, it is transferred by the army to the civilian authority and becomes a civilian village.

Gadna, the abbreviation for Gedudei No'ar ("Youth

Druze members of the Israel Border Police, 1965. Courtesy Government Press Office, Tel Aviv.

Battalions"), deals with premilitary training of Israel youth in and out of school. The organization is essentially educational in nature, although it provides its members with some basic military training in various arms. Members of Gadna assist in afforestation projects, archaeological excavations, and border kibbutzim. Gadna is designed to develop a spirit of constructive patriotism and to identify the army primarily with construction and not with destruction.

Ḥen (Ḥeil Nashim; "Women's Army") is essentially an auxiliary military organization supporting the armed forces in many fields. It supplies women for duties in communications, hospitals, teaching duties, and many other headquarters functions, and thus relieves the men of the country for active combat.

The Minorities in the IDF. Members of the minorities may, under certain circumstances, volunteer for service in the IDF and in the Border Police. The Border Police Force

Border police on an exercise, January 1965. Courtesy Government Press Office, Tel Aviv.

is completely integrated between Jews and Druze, and many Druze have attained officer rank. The Druze community is now liable for conscription into the IDF in the same manner as members of the Jewish community. Until a few years ago this community was permitted to volunteer for service, but at the specific request of the Druze community itself the National Service Law imposing conscription was applied to its members. Bedouin and members of the Christian Arab community may volunteer for service. The IDF includes a Minorities Unit in which Druze and Christian Arabs serve. A certain percentage of members of the unit are Jewish, and the unit has served with distinction in many border operations.

Army Corps. Troops serving in the IDF are assigned to various Army corps, which are responsible for the professional and technical training of officers and the enlisted men and the development of equipment and the doctrines of the various arms. These corps include the air force, navy, infantry, armor, artillery, engineers, paratroops, signals and communications, intelligence, ordnance, supply, medical, military police, general service corps, and Naḥal. The formations directly under the General Staff are the regional commands, the navy and the air force, and the armored forces. The basic formation in the IDF is the brigade group. Any number of brigade groups can be combined under the command of divisional groupings in time of war.

Regional Defense. The static defense of the country is based on a regional defense system that is controlled by a special staff in the headquarters of the regional command. Various border villages are trained as defensive localities. The villages are controlled by an area headquarters, which in turn is under command of a district headquarters, which is controlled by the special staff for regional defense in command headquarters. The purpose of this organization is to ensure that the armed forces will be relieved of the task of static defense and will be thus free to engage the enemy in battle. The air force is responsible for the entire air defense of the country, and the navy is responsible for all aspects of coastal defense.

TRAINING. The armed forces support a training establishment that provides for every form of training in all arms of service, from the initial training of a private up to and including Command General Staff School. A number of army personnel are sent abroad annually for training. The basic theme of the training given to the personnel of the IDF emphasises the necessity for personal initiative and the importance of the officers and N.C.O.s displaying personal example in leadership. Great emphasis in all facets of leadership training is placed on this point and on the fact that the officer must always lead his men into battle. In fact, these values have developed into a living tradition of which the IDF is very proud. The IDF has assisted the training of armies in Asia, South America, and Africa, particularly in fields such as commando and parachute training and specific programs such as Naḥal and Gadna.

Education in the Forces. The IDF exercises a profound educational influence not only on the youth during their national service but also on those who come in contact with the army during periods of reserve duty. Owing to the close relationship between army and people, which became even closer during the years of almost continuous military activity following the Six-Day War, each had a considerable influence on the other. The IDF's educational work is of particular importance for new immigrants, for whom it is often a basic training in citizenship.

There are three main branches under the control of the Chief Education Officer: Education and Culture; Training and Information; Entertainment. The primary responsiblilty for regular educational and cultural activity rests on officers and N.C.O.s, who are trained for the task at the Military College of Education and the Educational Training Institute respectively, and provided with topical printed material. The IDF publishes an illustrated weekly of current events *Ba-Mahaneh*, and runs a radio program, Gallei Zahal, which "sandwiches" news, information, reportage, and comment between layers of popular music and entertainment. Both are served by army reporters with the troops.

All soldiers who do not have a basic knowledge of Hebrew must study the language in the normal course of their training and service, as well as at special intensive courses. Those who have not completed elementary education (eight years' study) attend three-month courses in Hebrew, history, geography, civics, arithmetic and geometry, nature study, and army history at the Army Education School (the Marcus Camp) at the end of their national service, receiving certificates recognized by the Ministry of Education and Culture. Optional post-primary courses, mainly for regular army men, prepare them for the official matriculation certificate. There are also correspondence courses, which can be taken during periods of active service.

The IDF publishes a wide variety of brochures and books on various regions and sectors, Diaspora Jewry, history of Israel, etc., and a series of low-priced, small paperbacks of Hebrew and translated fiction, called 89

"Sifriyyat Tarmil" ("Knapsack Library"). Soldiers in camps and at the front are supplied with daily newspapers, books, games, radio and, wherever possible, TV. Films are shown about twice a week and performances are given by the seven army entertainment troupes, which may split up into smaller teams to visit outlying positions. Civilian actors and entertainers perform frequently for soldiers at the front, sometimes in the framework of reserve service.

ARMS PURCHASE AND MANUFACTURE. From the early days the IDF was dependent to no small degree for arms supplies on foreign sources. The story of *"Rekhesh"*—as the "acquisition" of arms was called from the clandestine Haganah period and immediately after the establishment of the State—is a thrilling one. The first major arms purchase directly affecting the future army of Israel was that from Czechoslovakia in 1948, which included rifles, machine guns, and, later, Messerschmitt fighter planes. At the same time arms were purchased in France and from the surplus markets of the United States as well as those of many other countries. Until the British left the arms were smuggled into Palestine despite a British embargo. Supplies continued to arrive after the establishment of the State, primarily from the military surplus markets of the world.

In 1952, Israel formally signed an agreement with the United States government allowing for reimbursable military aid under Section 408E of the Mutual Security Act, but the U.S. remained a very small supplier. Israel's first jet aircraft, Meteors, were supplied by Britain, which also became in due course a major supplier of naval equipment, primarily destroyers and submarines. The 1950s saw the development of a special relationship between Israel and France, which became Israel's major arms supplier, providing aircraft, armor, and artillery. France remained Israel's main supplier of arms—above all, of modern jet aircraft—until June 2, 1967, when an embargo on the sale of arms to Israel was imposed by General de Gaulle.

The United States involvement in the supply of arms to Israel grew in the 1960s, with the supply, first, of Hawk ground-to-air missiles and, later, of Patton M 48 tanks, which together with British-supplied Centurion tanks constituted Israel's armored force. The United States became a major supplier of aircraft to Israel only after the Six-Day War and following the French embargo. U.S. supplies, which included F-4 Phantom fighter bombers and A-4 Skyhawk fighter bombers, were designed to offset the massive supply of arms by the Soviet Union to the Egyptian and Syrian forces. During and after the Yom Kippur War, U.S. arms supplies were of crucial importance for Israel's defense.

From the earliest days Israel made efforts to develop her own arms industry and in the course of years a major industry, capable of supplying most of the small arms and ammunition requirements of the IDF, as well as other types, was established. Parallel to this, Israel Aircraft Industries was established with a large electronic manufacturing component capable of assembling jet trainers and maintaining all the types of aircraft in service in the Israel Air Force.

Uniforms. The first IDF uniforms (1948) were to a large degree identical with those of the British army during World War II, though the symbols of rank were different. Over the years, the IDF developed uniforms that specifically answer to its needs, but influences of style from Western armies (Britain and the United States) are still noticeable. The basic colors of the winter uniform—dark khaki (army), blue-gray (air force), and dark blue (navy)—are of "Anglo-Saxon" origin, as are the beige and white of the summer uniforms (British origin). The official dress uniform has been influenced to a large degree by the United States; the cut of the daily uniforms and caps, however, generally follows the British model: the black and red berets of the IDF follow the example of the British armored and paratroop corps, while the combat helmets follow the American model. The IDF nonetheless aims toward developing an original style of uniform, especially for the women soldiers. The symbols of rank for N.C.O.s are mostly original (straight horizontal stripes in place of the angular stripes in Britain and America); in the lower ranks of commissioned officers, American influence is felt somewhat; and in the higher ranks (major and up), British influence is distinguishable.

Part Four:

ASPECTS OF PUBLIC LIFE

1 POLITICAL LIFE AND PARTIES

Introduction. There was lively political activity among the Jews in the Land of Israel from the early days of Zionist settlement, and especially since the early 1900s, when the first parties with a comprehensive political program were established by the labor pioneers. These were followed by other groups, such as the religious Zionists and, in the 1920s, the middle class (eventually represented mainly by the General Zionists), and the maximalist Revisionist movement. Most of the parties and their ideologies had originated in the Diaspora. In the absence of a sovereign parliament, the parties aimed at influencing the policies of such major *yishuv* and Zionist bodies as the Histadrut, the Va'ad Le'ummi, and the Zionist Executive, as well as local councils and municipalities, through which the *yishuv* was able to act as a national entity, guiding its own destinies and striving for independence during the Mandate period. Most parties functioned on more than the political level, engaging in a variety of independent activities—social services, housing, education, and the establishment of new settlements—generally with the aid of sister organizations abroad.

It was largely due to the existence of these parties, which had conducted intensive political activities for almost half a century, including periodical elections by popular vote, that independent Israel (1948) was able to proceed immediately to the establishment of an orderly and democratic parliamentary system. After the first Knesset elections in 1949, the main concern of the parties was to gain governmental and municipal power, but they continued their activities on the world Zionist scene and maintained many of their independent social and economic services, while the labor parties and, later, the others—with the exception of the religious ones—continued to contend for control of the Histadrut.

Despite the quadrupling of the Jewish population between 1948 and 1970, mainly by immigration, new political groupings based on "ethnic" or communal lines failed to gain substantial representation, and new immigrants generally joined the existing parties without notably changing their relative strengths. Mergers and alliances gradually reduced the number of parties. All Israel cabinets have been based on coalitions, in which Mapai (from 1968 the united Israel Labor Party) has held the central position, supported by varying combinations of left-wing, religious, and non-Socialist parties. Arab electors have been represented in the Knesset by regional lists allied with Labor and by individual members of the Mapam and Communist factions.

Political parties in independent Israel may be divided into the following groups:

In the labor movement, the largest was Mapai, founded in 1930 by the amalgamation of smaller groups, which retained its predominance even after the secession of the left-wing Aḥdut ha-Avodah in 1944. In 1965 the two parties combined in an electoral and parliamentary alliance (known as the Alignment), but at the same time a section under the leadership of former Premier David Ben-Gurion split off under the name of Rafi. After the Six-Day War all three reunited to form the Israel Labor Party, but each retained a measure of autonomony and jealously guarded its share in cabinet posts, Knesset seats, and other positions. In 1948 the Ha-Shomer ha-Ẓa'ir Kibbutz and youth movement, which had remained outside the 1930 merger, joined with Aḥdut ha-Avodah to form Mapam, the United Workers' Party, retaining the name after Aḥdut ha-Avodah seceded in 1954. In 1969 Mapam joined with the Israel Labor Party in a new Alignment. The Labor-Mapam Alignment, which initially had 67 seats in the Knesset out of 120 (together with its affiliated local Arab lists) when it was founded, declined to 60 in 1969 and 54 in 1973, but still remained the largest, and key grouping.

On the other side of the political spectrum, three parties at first competed with each other and with the labor parties. These were: Herut, a strongly nationalist opposition to Mapai predominance; the General Zionists, who appealed mainly to middle-class electors and business men; and a small Progressive Party, which generally cooperated with Mapai. General Zionists and Progressives merged in 1961 to form the Liberal Party, but split in 1965 when the majority joined with Herut to form Gahal, the Herut-Liberal Bloc, the minority becoming the Independent Liberal Party. In 1973 Gahal combined with three smaller groups to form the Likkud (Union), which won 39 seats in that year's elections, constituting for the first time a serious challenge to Labor.

Four religious parties, Mizrachi (religious Zionists) and Agudat Israel (orthodox non-Zionists), each with its labor wing, combined to form the Religious Front for the first parliamentary elections in 1949, which split in 1951. In 1956 the Mizrachi merged with its labor offshoot, which was larger than the parent body, to form the National Religious Party (Mafdal), which partnered Mapai and Labor in almost every coalition government; the Agudah parties remained in opposition most of the time.

The Israel Communist Party (Maki), which derived most of its support from the Arab population, split in 1965 into Rakah (New Communist List), which continued its anti-Zionist line and Maki, which retained the name but gradually abandoned anti-Zionism and in 1973 merged with leftist groups to form Moked.

In addition, small factions arose from time to time but either did not succeed in winning a single seat at elections, disappeared from the scene after a while, or merged into larger groupings. Thus, while there were 14 parties or factions at the end of the Seventh Knesset, there were eight at the beginning of the Eighth, elected in 1973. The two largest units, the Alignment and the Likkud, had 93 out of the 120 seats between them and the next-largest party, the National Religious Party, had 10, leaving four parties with 3–5 seats each and one with a single seat.

Early Parties—1900–1918. The first parties in the new *yishuv* were founded in the first decade of the 20th century by newcomers belonging to the Second Aliyah. Ha-Po'el ha-Za'ir ("the young worker," as distinct from the "old workers" of the First Aliyah, most of whom had become overseers or private farmers), led by Yosef Aharonovitz, Yosef Vitkin, and Yosef Sprinzak, was founded in 1905. Po'alei Zion, a Socialist Zionist party which originated in Russia, Austria, and other countries, was established in the Land of Israel in 1906. Among its leaders were Izhak Ben-Zvi, David Ben-Gurion, and Yizhak Tabenkin. Its aim was "to create a Jewish society based on socialist foundations in the Land of Israel," and the method it envisaged was "an unremitting class struggle." Ha-Po'el ha-Za'ir rejected the class struggle on the ground that the Jewish society and economy in Palestine were still in the precapitalist stage. "Our interest—to create a Jewish center in the Land of Israel—and the class struggle are a contradiction in terms," wrote Aharonovitz. The first article in the Ha-Po'el ha-Za'ir program called for "the conquest of all branches of work" (Hebrew *kibbush avodah*, meaning that Jewish workers should do even menial work themselves, not leaving manual effort to non-Jews). A group of nonparty workers, notably Berl Katznelson and David Remez, opposed the division into two parties and called for labor unity.

The parties engaged in practical work as well as theoretical discussion. New arrivals in Jaffa often found that they had to choose between two hotels, one for each party. But there was little difference in their day-to-day lives and their practical approach to problems. Both groups tried to remove the obstacles to Jewish immigration, win rights of employment for Jewish workers in the Jewish

farms and orange groves, and improve working conditions.

Ha-Po'el ha-Ẓa'ir group at the party's fourth general meeting in Jaffa, 1908. Courtesy Central Zionist Archives, Jerusalem. Photo Ben Dov, Jerusalem.

At its first conference in Jaffa, at the beginning of 1907, Po'alei Zion proclaimed its aspiration for "political independence for the Jewish people in this country," and decided to send an independent faction of delegates to the Zionist Congress. It was associated almost from the first with the Po'alei Zion world movement, whereas Ha-Po'el ha-Ẓa'ir established ties with the Ẓe'irei Zion movement in the Diaspora only in 1913.

In 1908 a controversy broke out in Ha-Po'el ha-Ẓa'ir on the question of how to encourage the workers to remain on the land. At a special conference Vitkin called for the establishment of workers' small holdings near the moshavot to enable them to become independent cultivators instead of mere agricultural laborers. The "conquest of labor," he declared, must be accompanied by the "conquest of the soil." He was opposed by Aharonovitz, who believed that the 99 only way to increase the Jewish population was to create an agricultural proletariat, working as wage earners on private farms, and leave the "conquest of the soil" to the Zionist Organization. The issue was ultimately decided by the exigencies of life: members of Ha-Po'el ha-Za'ir were among the founders of Deganyah, the first kevuzah, and Nahalal, the first moshav, while Po'alei Zion, despite its class-war doctrine, devoted most of its energies to constructive activities, including the establishment of labor exchanges, cooperative groups, and mutual aid institutions.

A bureau of the religious Mizrachi Party, which had been a part of the World Zionist Organization since 1902, was set up in the Land of Israel in 1912, but did not become active until after the end of World War I. Its labor wing, Ha-Po'el ha-Mizrachi, was founded in 1922. The basic principle of the movement was: "The Land of Israel for the People of Israel in accordance with the Torah of Israel." The non-Zionist Orthodox Agudat Israel, which opposed the secular organization of the *yishuv*, was also established in the Land of Israel in 1912, simultaneously with the founding of its parent world organization.

Steps Toward Labor Unity. Toward the end of World War I, the nonparty labor group led by Berl Katznelson appealed for an end to the rivalry between the two workers' parties, so that labor could exert its full influence in the development of the *yishuv*. It called for the establishment of an all-inclusive labor organization which would be a trade union as well as a political party, establishing settlements and cooperatives, helping new immigrants, and providing social services for its members. At a unity conference in February 1919, Po'alei Zion and the nonparty group, with the support of a majority of the Agricultural Workers' Federation, formed Ahdut ha-Avodah ("unity of labor"). Ha-Po'el ha-Za'ir refused to join, mainly because the new organization described itself as "a branch of the socialist labor movement in the world." To an attack on these grounds by A. D. Gordon, Joseph Hayyim Brenner replied that although the critics rejected socialism, they followed its principles in daily life. Ha-Po'el ha-Za'ir also believed in building up small, closely knit communes, while Ahdut ha-Avodah aimed at developing a mass movement.

To diminish the growing rivalry between them, Joseph Trumpeldor, a leading figure of the Second Aliyah, proposed the establishment of a neutral, independent trade union federation to which both would be affiliated. His initiative bore fruit after his tragic death, when the organization he envisaged, the Histadrut, was established at a labor movement conference in Haifa in December 1920. The 4,433 registered members elected 38 delegates from Ahdut ha-Avodah, 27 from Ha-Po'el ha-Za'ir, 16 from the New Immigrants list representing He-Halutz, Ha-Shomer ha-Za'ir, and others, and six from the extreme leftist Mifleget Po'alim Sozialistim ("Socialist Workers' Party"), nicknamed "Mopsim," which had split off from Po'alei Zion when Ahdut ha-Avodah was formed.

Immediately after the end of World War I, preparations were made for the establishment of an autonomous, democratically elected body to organize the *yishuv* and represent it in dealings with the authorities. A provisional committee held three sessions in 1918 and 1919, the first representing only Tel Aviv and its surroundings, the second Jerusalem as well, and the third consisting of delegates from all parts of the country. On April 19, 1920, elections were held to an Asefat Ha-Nivharim (Elected Assembly). In addition to the workers' parties and Mizrachi, a variety of communal, religious, vocational, and local groups sought representation and nineteen lists of candidates were submitted. Each list received one delegate for every 80 votes polled; 77% of the electors voted and 314 delegates were elected. Ahdut ha-Avodah, with 70 delegates, was the largest group; next came the Sephardi Union with 54, Ha-Po'el ha-Za'ir with 41, the Farmers' Union with 16, the Progressive Party (Mitkaddemim) with 13, the Yemenites with 12, two Mizrachi lists with a total of 11, and 11 other groups with a total of 46 places. An additional 51 delegates were chosen at separate polls by Orthodox men, who refused to participate in elections in which women had the franchise.

At the Assembly's first session, in October 1920, the 20 factions combined into three wings: right, consisting of the oriental Jews and the religious groups; left, composed of the two labor parties; and center, consisting of the other groups. The Assembly elected a Va'ad Le'ummi (national council) of 36, comprising Aḥdut ha-Avodah 8, Sephardim 6, Ha-Po'el ha-Ẓa'ir 5, Orthodox 5, Progressives 3, Farmers 2, Yemenites 2, Mizrachi and Clerks 1 each. Meir Dizengoff, Vladimir Jabotinsky, Haim Margolis-Kalvaryski, and David Yellin were elected on a personal basis. The Va'ad Le'ummi was headed by a presidium of three, assisted by an executive council whose membership varied from 7 to 14.

The second session of the first Assembly, which was scheduled for May 1921, did not take place until the following March, because of the May riots and their aftermath, the categorical refusal of the Orthodox delegates to participate as long as women were allowed to vote, and the Sephardim's and Farmers' objections to the proposed self-taxation system. Further negotiations with these groups, as well as fruitless attempts to obtain official recognition by the Mandatory government, held up the convening of the third session until June 1925. Despite prolonged efforts to solve the problem of women's suffrage, the Orthodox and Mizrachi delegates did not attend the second and third sessions, and it was not until the eve of the next elections that the Mizrachi agreed to participate, with the Orthodox maintaining their boycott.

At the elections to the second Assembly, held on December 6, 1925, the Palestine branch of the Revisionist Organization, led by Jabotinsky, made its first appearance in the politics of the *yishuv*, gaining 15 seats out of 201. The labor parties increased their relative strength, while the middle class and the religious Jews became even more fragmented than before. Aḥdut ha-Avodah had 54 seats, Ha-Po'el ha-Ẓa'ir 30, Sephardim and oriental groups 19,

Meeting of Aḥdut ha-Avodah and Ha-Po'el ha-Ẓa'ir, merging to form Mapai, 1930. Courtesy Central Zionist Archives, Jerusalem.

five Mizrachi lists, together, 19, the Women's Equal Rights Association 13, and the Agricultural Bloc 9. A "working-class" list, with 6 seats, reflected the influence of the Palestine Communist Party (P.K.P.), which had been formed illegally in 1921 by members of the "Mopsim" and other groups. The Yemenites, alleging discrimination, boycotted the elections, but were later permitted to elect 20 additional delegates of their own. The second Assembly elected a Va'ad Le'ummi of 38: 18 representing the United Bloc (Mizrachi, Sephardim, Yemenites, Farmers, and others), 9 for Aḥdut ha-Avodah, 5 for Ha-Po'el ha-Ẓa'ir, and 2 each for Women, Revisionists, and the Democratic group.

Strengthening of the Political Parties. The high commissioner's ratification of the regulations for Keneset Yisrael, officially recognizing its representative bodies, the Asefat ha-Nivḥarim and the Va'ad Le'ummi, was announced on Jan. 1, 1928, but it took more than two years to draft the election rules and to prepare a register of all the members of 103 the Jewish community as prescribed by the regulations. The total number of Assembly members was fixed at 71, with the electors divided into three colleges, or curiae: Ashkenazim, with 53 delegates, Sephardim 15, and Yemenites 3. Each elector was allowed to vote only in his own college.

In 1930 Aḥdut ha-Avodah and Ha-Po'el ha-Za'ir merged to form Mapai (Mifleget Po'alei Erez Israel—"Palestine labor party"), which immediately became the strongest political force in the *yishuv*. The Left Po'alei Zion and Ha-Shomer ha-Za'ir remained outside the merger.

At the elections to the third Assembly, on Jan. 5, 1931, Mapai, with 27 delegates, together with 4 Sephardi Labor, was by far the strongest party. The Revisionists, with 16, including 5 Sephardim, also increased their strength considerably, followed by the Sephardim (general) with 6, Mizrachi and Ha-Po'el ha-Mizrachi 5, and General Zionists 4. The Farmers refused to participate in the elections when their demand for three guaranteed seats was refused and the Communists did not win a place. In the 23-member Va'ad Le'ummi, Mapai had 11 members, Sephardim 4, Mizrachi 3, General Zionists 3, Women 1, and Yemenites 1. The Revisionists refused to join the Va'ad Le'ummi because of dissatisfaction with the Assembly's political decisions, but were given 5 seats in the following year, leaving Mapai with 10 seats and the three other main parties with 2 each.

The third Assembly lasted for over 13 years, as elections were repeatedly postponed because of recurrent Arab violence, continuous political tension, and then the outbreak of World War II. With the growth of the *yishuv*, the parties in Palestine, especially Mapai, became the dominant influence in the Jewish Agency. Chaim Arlosoroff, named head of the Jewish Agency political department in 1931, was succeeded, after his assassination in 1933, by Moshe Shertok (Sharett). David Ben-Gurion became chairman of the executive in 1935.

While the Jewish Agency was responsible for major
political affairs, politics played a prominent role in most of

the Assembly's 18 sessions. Jewish Agency representatives reported regularly to the Assembly and the Va'ad Le'ummi, political resolutions were generally drafted in close cooperation between the two bodies, and representations to the British authorities were often submitted jointly. Other issues were: defense against Arab violence; the utilization of national funds; the allocation of immigration certificates; education; trade union policy and the right to strike; the role of the Histadrut in the establishment of new settlements and economic enterprises; and the activities of local authorities and local councils.

Most political parties not only worked in the Va'ad Le'ummi, the Jewish Agency, the local authorities, and the Histadrut, but also established agricultural settlements, schools, housing projects, industries, transport, and service cooperatives, and other constructive enterprises, either independently or through affiliated economic bodies. Almost all the parties organized their own youth movements. Conflicting party influences were also apparent in the ranks of the Haganah.

The most outspoken opposition to the official policies of the Jewish Agency and the *yishuv* came from the Revisionists, who called on the Zionist movement to proclaim the establishment of a Jewish state on both banks of the Jordan as the ultimate aim of Zionism. They accused Chaim Weizmann and his labor supporters of compromising with the British government, alleged that the Executive discriminated against middle-class immigrants, opposed the system of general, religious and labor "trends" in education and demanded compulsory arbitration in labor disputes. Tension mounted after the murder of Arlosoroff in 1933, when two Revisionists were accused of the crime. An agreement reached in the following year by Ben-Gurion and Jabotinsky on a modus vivendi in labor relations was rejected, after a referendum, by the members of the Histadrut. Controversy grew still more heated after the majority of Revisionists left the World Zionist Organization in 1935, and a minority, refusing to leave. founded the Jewish State Party.

Revisionist criticism of Labor's economic and social policies was, on the whole, supported by the right wing of the General Zionists. In 1935 the General Zionists split into the Federation (Hitaḥadut) and the Union (Berit) of General Zionists, known, respectively, as the A and B Factions. The A group, with Weizmann as its leader, cooperated with Labor. So did Mizrachi and Ha-Po'el ha-Mizrachi, though they frequently opposed Mapai on religious and educational issues. On the left, Ha-Shomer ha-Ẓa'ir, which gradually became more active as a political party, demanded joint organization of Jewish and Arab workers and greater efforts to reach an agreement with the Arabs, while also endorsing the principle of immigration to the full economic absorptive capacity of the country. Despite party differences, there was a large measure of common ground on such practical issues as immigration, settlement on the land, defense, and opposition to the restrictive policies of the Mandatory government. An exception was the anti-Zionist Palestine Communist Party, which made largely unsuccessful efforts to recruit Arab members and in 1936–39 openly supported the Arab revolt and Arab terrorism against the Jews. In 1939 it split up into separate Jewish and Arab groups.

The 1937 Peel Commission's proposal for the partition of Palestine into two states, Jewish and Arab, and a British zone, aroused controversy that largely cut across party lines, particularly in Mapai and in both factions of the General Zionists. While the majority in these parties was prepared, in principle, to consider partition, Berl Katznelson of Mapai and Menahem Ussishkin of the General Zionists B were categorically opposed. The Revisionists were against partition on political grounds and the Mizrachi on religious grounds, while Ha-Shomer ha-Ẓa'ir advocated the establishment of Palestine as a binational state. The latter joined forces on the issue of Arab-Jewish relations with a small nonparty group, founded as Berit Shalom ("Peace Alliance") in 1925 and later called

Kedmah Mizraḥah (from 1936), the League for Jewish-Arab Understanding (from 1939), and Iḥud (from 1942). Among its leaders were Rabbi Binyamin (Radler-Feldman), Haim Margolis-Kalvaryski, Judah L. Magnes, and Martin Buber. Bitter, occasionally violent, controversy arose over defense policy during the Arab riots of 1936–39. The Revisionists rejected the Haganah's policy of *havlagah* ("restraint"); their members were the backbone of the Irgun Zeva'i Le'ummi, which carried out reprisals against the Arabs and engaged in guerrilla activity against the British forces.

During World War II, after the abandonment of partition by the British and the adoption of the White Paper Policy, opinion in the Zionist movement crystallized around the Biltmore Program. This plan, calling for the establishment of Palestine as "a Jewish Commonwealth integrated in the structure of the new democratic world," was approved by the Inner Zionist General Council on Nov. 10, 1942, by 21 votes to 4, with 3 abstentions. The program was supported by Mapai, the General Zionists, and Mizrachi, and opposed by Ha-Shomer ha-Za'ir, which called for political parity of Jews and Arabs, and by the Left Po'alei Zion. The abstentions came from representatives of Si'ah Bet (the "B Faction" of Mapai), who insisted on a demand for Jewish rights in the whole of Palestine.

A new party, Aliyah Ḥadashah, mainly representing recent immigrants from Germany and Central Europe, founded in 1942, favored a continuation of the British Mandate and a further attempt to reach an agreement with the Arabs. The struggle conducted within Mapai by Si'ah Bet for the right to fight for its independent left wing views came to a head at the Mapai conference at Kefar Vitkin in October 1942, with a majority decision to prohibit factions within the party. In May 1944 Si'ah Bet formed a new party, Ha-Tenu'ah le-Aḥdut ha-Avodah, which amalgamated with Ha-Shomer ha-Za'ir and the Left Po'alei Zion in January 1948 to form Mapam (Mifleget ha-Po'alim ha-Me'uḥedet: "united workers' party"). 107

The fourth Asefat ha-Nivḥarim was elected on August 1, 1944. The Revisionists, General Zionists B, and Sephardim boycotted the elections because their demands for changes in the electoral system were refused, while Agudat Israel maintained its ban. However, 67% of the vastly increased electorate of 300,000 went to the polls (see Table).

Labor continued to dominate the Va'ad Le'ummi: of 42 members, 15 were from Mapai, and eight from the other two left-wing parties, while Izhak Ben-Zvi and David Remez were elected president and chairman respectively. During the subsequent period, major political and defense issues overshadowed all others. Interparty conflict was reflected in the dissensions between the Haganah, which was controlled by the Jewish Agency, and the largely Revisionist Irgun Ẓeva'i Le'ummi. Left-wing predominance in the Palmaḥ, which was part of the Haganah, also gave rise to occasional disagreements.

When the Palestine problem was submitted to the United Nations (1947), however, the majority of the yishuv and the Zionist movement was united in support of the demand for the establishment of a Jewish State, even in part of the country, though the Revisionists pressed for their maximalist program and Ha-Shomer ha-Ẓa'ir continued to advocate a binational state. After the U.N. Special Committee on Palestine (UNSCOP) issued its report recommending the establishment in Palestine of both a Jewish and an Arab state, almost all parties (including the Communists after the U.S.S.R. had expressed its support for partition) collaborated in the effort to carry out the transition to independence.

Transition to Statehood. On April 12, 1948, the Zionist General Council laid the foundations for the self-governing institutions of the Jewish State by appointing a provisional legislature, called "The Thirty-Seven," or Mo'eẓet ha-Am (people's council), and an executive called "The Thirteen" or Minhelet ha-Am (people's administration). Seats were allocated according to the existing strengths of the parties. The people's council consisted of the 14 members of the executive of the Va'ad Le'ummi, the 11 Palestine members of the Jewish Agency executive, and 12 delegates from parties not represented on either (Sephardim, Revisionists, Agudat Israel, and Communists). Its party composition was 10 Mapai, 6 General Zionists, 5 Ha-Po'el ha-Mizrachi and Mizrachi, 5 Mapam, 3 Agudat Israel, 3 Revisionists, and 1 each representing Communists, WIZO (Women's International Zionist Organization), Aliyah Ḥadashah, Sephardim, and Yemenites. Chaim Weizmann was the president of the council and its 38th member. For the first time, Agudat Israel and the Communists were represented on the governing bodies of the *yishuv*.

On May 14 the people's council and the people's administration became respectively the provisional council of state and the provisional government of the independent State of Israel. The Revisionists and Communists were in opposition. The provisional government (see below) set the basic pattern for Israel's coalition cabinets. When a new one was formed, an attempt was generally made to include representatives of the political spectrum from the General Zionists on the right to Mapam on the left. Usually, however, one or another extreme could not be fitted in; it was only between 1955 and 1959 that both participated at the same time. Not until the formation of the "Government of National Union" in 1967, on the eve of the Six-Day War, was the spectrum extended to include a representative of the Jabotinsky camp (former Revisionists and IZL).

In June 1948 Menahem Begin, commander of the Irgun Zeva'i Le'ummi, launched the Ḥerut ("Freedom") movement as its political successor. At a Revisionist Party convention in December, there was a split, the great majority of the delegates joining the new party while the veteran leaders retained the Revisionist label. Both sections submitted lists at the elections. The General Zionists had split in August, the B group retaining the name and the A group, together with Aliyah Ḥadashah and Ha-Oved ha-Ziyyoni, forming the new Progressive Party in the following month. During the War of Independence of 1948,

Representation of Parties in the Elected Assemblies

	First	Second	Third	Fourth
Date of elections	April 19, 1920	Dec. 6, 1925	Jan. 5, 1931	Aug. 1, 1944
Number of electors	28,765	64,764	89,656	300,018
Percentage of votes cast	77%	57%	56%	67%
Number of lists represented	20	25	14	18
Composition of delegates				
Aḥdut ha-Avodah	70	54	27[6]	63[6]
Ha-po'el ha-Ẓa'ir	41	30		63
Other labor groups	——	6	7[7]	40[9]
Sephardim	54	19	6	——
Other oriental communities	18	21[3]	3	6
Orthodox	51[1]	——	——	——
Mizrachi groups	11	19[4]	5	24
Other religious groups	2	——	——	3
Revisionists	——	15	16[8]	——
Farmers	16	9		
Women's groups	5	14	3	4
General Zionists	——	——	4	7
Other groups	46[2]	34[5]	——	24[10]
Total	314	221	71	171

[1] Elected at separate polls.
[2] Eight lists.
[3] Including 20 Yemenites elected at separate polls.
[4] Five lists.
[5] Eleven lists.
[6] Mapai.
[7] Including four Sephardi Labor.
[8] Including five Sephardi Revisionists.
[9] Ha-Shomer ha-Ẓa'ir—21; Le-Aḥdut ha-Avodah—16; Popular Democrats (Communists)—3.
[10] Including 18 Aliyah Ḥadashah.

internal political problems remained in the background, and party differences found expression mainly in the fields of military and foreign policy. Ḥerut denounced Ben-Gurion's measures against the Irgun Ẓeva'i Le'ummi, especially in connection with the Altalena affair, which also gave

rise to uneasiness among the General Zionists and Mizrachi, while Mapam was disturbed by the abolition of the Palmaḥ high command.

The First Knesset—1949-51. After the elections to the constituent assembly (the First Knesset), Ben-Gurion was called upon by President Weizmann to form the first regular government. Mapai, with 46 seats out of 120, was more than twice as large as the next—Mapam, with 19—but it could not govern alone. On the other hand, no possible combination of right-wing or center parties could command a majority without it, since Ḥerut, the General Zionists, the United Religious Front, and the Progressives had only 42 seats among them. Ben-Gurion started negotiations with all the parties represented in the provisional government on the allocation of portfolios and the policies to be pursued by the new cabinet, but could not meet all the demands of Mapam and the General Zionists. After two weeks' negotiations, he formed a cabinet of 12: seven Mapai and one each from Mizrachi, Ha-Po'el ha-Mizrachi, Agudat Israel, Progressives, and Sephardim. He himself, along with Sharett, Rosenblueth, Kaplan, Remez, Maimon, Shapira, Levin, and Shitrit, retained the posts they had held in the provisional government. Dov (Bernard) Joseph took over Supply and Rationing; Golda Meyerson (Meir), Labor and National Insurance; and Zalman Shazar (Rubashov), Education and Culture. The portfolios of Agriculture, Commerce and Industry, and Health were held in reserve in the hope that Mapam and the General Zionists might join the government later; in the meantime, they were entrusted to Joseph, Kaplan, and Shapira respectively. The government's composition and program were approved by 73 votes to 45. An alliance between Mapai, Mizrachi and Ha-Po'el ha-Mizrachi (later National Religious Party), and the Progressives (later Independent Liberals) was to form the backbone of almost all subsequent governments.

During the succeeding months, interparty controversy centered on economic issues. The General Zionists and Ḥerut continued to urge greater freedom for private

Ministry	Minister	Party
Prime Minister and Defense	David Ben-Gurion	Mapai
Foreign Affairs	Moshe Shertok (Sharett)	Mapai
Finance	Eliezer Kaplan	Mapai
Transport and Communications	David Remez	Mapai
Commerce, Industry and Supply	Perez Bernstein	General Zionists
Interior	Yizḥak Gruenbaum	General Zionists
Labor and Construction	Mordekhai Bentov	Mapam
Agriculture	Aharon Zisling	Mapam
Justice	Felix Rosenblueth (Pinḥas Rosen)	Aliyah Ḥadashah
Religious Affairs and War Casualties	Yehudah Leib Fishman (Maimon)	Mizrachi
Immigration and Health	Moshe Shapira	Ha-Po'el ha-Mizrachi
Social Welfare	Yizḥak Meir Levin	Agudat Israel
Police and Minorities	Behor Shalom Shitrit	Sephardi

enterprise and denounced Dov Joseph's austerity policy. Mapam fought Mapai's policy of wage restraint in the Histadrut and actively supported street demonstrations by the unemployed and claims for higher wages in industry. There were also difficulties within the coalition. The Compulsory Education Law of September 1949 confirmed the division of the educational system into four trends: General, Labor, Mizrachi, and Agudat Israel. However, the system was too cumbersome to be implemented in the immigrant camps and *ma'barot* (transitional settlements), and the religious parties complained that the children of religious immigrants were, in fact, being given a nonreligious education.

In October 1950 Ben-Gurion proposed replacing the Ministry of Supply and Rationing with the ministries of Agriculture and of Commerce and Industry. The United Religious Front (URF) refused to agree unless their demands were met, and Ben-Gurion submitted his resignation. At the end of the month the URF withdrew their objections, on receiving assurance that steps would be taken to meet their main demands. Ben-Gurion formed a new cabinet, which received a vote of confidence on Nov. 1. Ya'akov Geri (nonparty) became minister of commerce and industry, and Pinḥas Lubianiker (Lavon), of Mapai, minister of agriculture, while Joseph was transferred to the portfolio of communications, and Remez replaced Shazar as minister of education and culture.

Despite interparty differences, there was general agreement on the policy of mass immigration and the ingathering of the exiles. The national consensus was reflected in the Law of Return, passed in July 1950, which recognized the right of every Jew to settle in Israel. Although it had been understood that the drafting of a constitution would be one of the Assembly's main tasks, Ben-Gurion, supported by his party, objected to the enactment of hard-and-fast constitutional rules during the transitional period of the ingathering of the exiles, while the United Religious Front refused to agree to any constitution not based on the authority of the Torah. In June 1950, after a full-dress debate, the Knesset decided to instruct the Law, Constitution, and Justice Committee to prepare a series of fundamental laws, which, when completed, would form the constitution of the state.

Growing popular dissatisfaction with supply shortages and strict rationing was reflected at the local authority elections in November 1950 by impressive General Zionist gains, mainly at Mapai's expense. When Remez announced that parents in the *ma'barot* who wished their children to receive a religious education would be allowed to choose not only Mizrachi or Agudat Israel schools, but also a newly created religious "sub-trend" in the Histadrut school system, the United Religious Front voted against the government. The government was defeated in the Knesset by 49 votes to 42 and was forced to resign.

The Second Knesset—1951–55. The elections, which took place on July 30, 1951, resulted in the expected gains by the General Zionists, who obtained 20 seats (later supplemented by the adherence of two Sephardim and one Yemenite). However, Mapai (which had been joined by another section of the Sephardim), while presumably losing middle-class votes, gained support at the expense of Mapam, whose seats declined from 19 to 15. Mapai's percentage of the votes actually rose to 37.3, compared with 35.7 in 1949, although its Knesset strength declined slightly to 45 because of a technical change in the election regulations. The greatest loser was Ḥerut, which dropped from 14 seats to eight (see Table below). The base of the new cabinet, which was presented on October 7, after two months' negotiations, was even narrower than the last: only Mapai, Mizrachi, and Ha-Po'el ha-Mizrachi were represented. The General Zionists broke off talks when Ben-Gurion refused to grant control over imports to their candidate for the portfolio of commerce and industry, and the Progressives would not participate without them.

The cabinet consisted of nine Mapai ministers, three from the religious parties, and one Sephardi. Perez Naftali became minister of economic coordination; Dov Joseph took over Commerce and Industry and, temporarily, Justice; Ben-Zion Dinaburg (Dinur) became minister of education and culture in succession to David Remez, who had recently died; Yosef Burg (Ha-Po'el ha-Mizrachi) and David Zevi Pinkas (Mizrachi) became ministers of health and communications respectively. In June 1952 Kaplan resigned from the Treasury owing to ill health, becoming deputy prime minister, and was succeeded by Levi Eshkol. Naftali became minister of agriculture, Lavon remained in the Cabinet as minister without portfolio, and Attorney General Haim Cohn took over the Ministry of Justice. At about this time, political controversy between Mapai

114

and Mapam members in the Ha-Kibbutz ha-Me'uḥad settlement movement grew so virulent that some of the kibbutzim split, the Mapai sections joining with Ḥever ha-Kevuẓot to form ʾhud ha-Kevuẓot ve-ha-Kibbutzim.

One of the most urgent problems with which the government had to deal was that of reparations from Germany. In January 1951 Israel had called upon the occupying powers to demand reparations from both parts of Germany. In September Chancellor Adenauer announced that the German Federal Republic was prepared to negotiate on the subject with representatives of the Jewish people and the State of Israel. On January 9, 1952, Ben-Gurion announced in the Knesset that "the Government of Israel regards it as its duty to make every appropriate effort, together with the representatives of world Jewry, to restore as quickly as possible to individual Jews and to the Jewish people the maximum amount of the plunder." At a mass demonstration in the center of Jerusalem, Ḥerut leader Menahem Begin proclaimed undying opposition to negotiations with Germany, declaring, "This will be a war for life and death." At the end of the meeting crowds of demonstrators made their way toward the Knesset building, throwing stones at the police guard, who responded with tear-gas bombs. Although some of the windows in the building were broken, the Knesset concluded its debate and decided, by the votes of the coalition and the Progressives, and against all the opposition parties, that the Foreign Affairs and Security Committee be empowered to decide on the action to be taken on the claim for reparations from Germany. A few days later the Committee authorized the government to open negotiations, which started on March 22 and were concluded on September 10.

Added to the reparations crisis was the growing dissatisfaction of Agudat Israel and its labor wing with the government's education policy and the proposal to institute national service for religious girls, previously exempted from conscription to the women's auxiliary services of the

Results of Knesset Elections (1949—65)(For 1969-73, see p. 143)

Party	First Jan, 25, 1949		Second July 30, 1951	
	%	Seats	%	Seats
Electorate	506,567		924,885	
Valid votes cast	434,684		787,492	
Mapai	35.7	46	37.3	45
Aḥdut ha—Avodah				
Mapam	14.7[1]	19	12.5[1]	15
Rafi[7]				
Ḥerut	11.5	14	6.6	8
Liberals[2]	{ 5.2	7	18.9	23
	{ 4.1	5	3.2	4
National Religious Party			8.3	10
Agudat Israel	12.2[3]	16		
Po'alei Agudat Israel			3.7[5]	5
Communists	3.5	4	4.0	5
Arabs (associated with Mapai)	3.0	2	4.7	5
Others	10.1	7[4]	0.8	——

[1] In 1949 and 1951 Mapam included Aḥdut ha-Avodah.
[2] Figures for the first four Knessets refer respectively to General Zionists and Progressives, who merged in 1961 to form the Liberal Party. See also notes 8 and 9.
[3] In 1949 these parties constituted the United Religious Front.
[4] Four Sephardim, one-Yemenite, one WIZO, and one "Fighters."
[5] In 1951, 1955, and 1959, these two parties conssituted the Torah Religious Front.
[6] Alignment (Mapai and Aḥdut ha-Avodah).

army. On September 19 their representatives resigned, leaving the government without a majority. Ben-Gurion approached the General Zionists at the end of the month and, after an interval, reopened negotiations at the beginning of December.

On December 23 a new coalition government of Mapai, the General Zionists, and the Progressives was approved in the Knesset by 63 votes to 24, and completed the next day by the inclusion of two Ha-Po'el ha-Mizrachi ministers. Mapai retained the premiership and the portfolios of

Third July 26, 1955		Fourth Nov. 3, 1959		Fifth Aug. 15, 1961		Sixth Nov. 2, 1965	
1,067,795		1,218,483		1,274,280		1,449,709	
853,219		969,337		1,006,964		1,206,728	
%	Seats	%	Seats	%	Seats	%	Seats
32.2	40	38.2	47	34.7	42	36.7[6]	45
8.2	10	6.0	7	6.6	8		
7.3	9	7.2	9	7.5	9	6 6	8
—	—	—	—	—	—	7.9	10
12.6	15	13.5	17	13.8	17 }	21.3[8]	
10.2	13	6.2	8 }	13.6	17 }		26[10]
4.4	5	4.6	6 }			3.8[9]	5
9.1	11	9.9	12	9.8	12	9.9	11
				3.7	4	3.3	4
4.7	6	4.7	6	1.9	2	1.8	2
4.5	6	2.8	3	4.2	5	3.4	4[11]
4.9	5	3.5	5	3.5	4	3.3	4
1.9	—	3.6	—	0.7	—	2.9	1[12]

[7] Rafi—Israel Labor List, formed in 1965 after a split in Mapai.
[8] Herut Liberal Bloc (Gahal).
[9] Independent Liberals.
[10] In 1967 three Herut Knesset members formed the independent Free Center faction.
[11] Three New Communist List (Rakah) and one Israel Communist Party (Maki).
[12] Ha-Olam ha-Zeh—New Force.

defense, foreign affairs, finance, education, labor, and agriculture, with Dov Joseph and Lavon as ministers without portfolio. For the General Zionists, Perez Bernstein took over the Ministry of Commerce and Industry, Israel Rokach the Interior, Yosef Saphir Communications, and Yosef Serlin Health. Pinḥas Rosen (Progressives) returned to the Ministry of Justice, while Moshe Shapira and Yosef Burg became minister of religious affairs and of social welfare, and minister of posts, respectively. The coalition agreement provided for the abolition of the "trend" system in education (with safe-guards for religious education), for income tax reforms, and for liberalization of export regulations.

Mapam was not invited to join the coalition. During this period it was deeply divided in its attitude to the Slansky trial in Prague, in which Mordekhai Oren, one of its members, was accused of espionage. Two former members of Le-Aḥdut ha-Avodah seceded in February 1953 and established a separate parliamentary faction, while a group led by Moshe Sneh was expelled for its pro-communist attitude and, after first forming the Left Faction, joined the Communist Party.

In the meantime, there had been a crisis in the election of a successor to President Weizmann, who died in November 1952. In the first two votes, a month later, no candidate received the absolute majority prescribed by law, and the deadlock was resolved only by Mapam switching its votes to Izhak Ben-Zvi, the veteran Mapai leader.

Apart from a short-lived crisis over the General Zionists' demand that the new State Education Law prohibit the flying of the red flag and the singing of the labor hymn in all schools, including those of the former Histadrut "trend," the coalition was reasonably harmonious. The education problem was solved by the law on free compulsory education, approved by the government in August 1953, which provided for the replacement of the "trends" by two types of schools: state and state-religious. Agudat Israel maintained its own schools independently, outside the state system, although with state assistance.

In November, Ben-Gurion startled the country by announcing his desire to retire from the premiership for a year or two for personal reasons, explaining that he needed a period of rest after the continuous tension of the past 23 years. He proposed that the existing coalition should continue, with Levi Eshkol as prime minister and Lavon as minister of defense. Eshkol refused the premiership and Mapai nominated Moshe Sharett for the post. Ben-Gurion announced (December 7) his retirement to his new kibbutz home at Sedeh Boker, where he engaged in a comprehensive study of the position of the armed forces and drafted proposals to meet the difficulties ahead. His last action before retirement was to appoint Moshe Dayan as chief of staff of the defense forces. The other parties submitted various demands as a condition for reforming the cabinet, and the new government, with Sharett as premier and foreign minister, Lavon as minister of defense, and Zalman Aranne as minister without portfolio, was not installed until January 26, 1954.

Sharett's term of office was marked by a number of developments which left their mark on Israel politics. In August, dissension in Mapam, due partly to the aftermath of the Prague trials, came to a head, and Le-Aḥdut ha-Avodah (which later dropped the prefix "Le") seceded. In September, the Mapai Central Council adopted Ben-Gurion's proposal to press for the replacement of proportional representation in Knesset elections by the single-member constituency system.

Most far-reaching in their effects, though not made public at the time, were disagreements between Sharett and Lavon over the execution of defense policy. The prime minister complained in private that he was not consulted in advance over reprisals against Arab border violence. Relations became insupportable when a security operation, never officially disclosed, came to a disastrous end while Dayan was abroad. Lavon disclaimed responsibility and blamed a senior officer for acting without his authority. An inquiry committee, consisting of Yiẓḥak Olshan, president of the Supreme Court, and Ya'akov Dori, former chief of staff, failed to reach a conclusion, and Lavon resigned. In response to Sharett's appeal, Ben-Gurion returned to the Cabinet as minister of defense, taking office on February 21, 1955. At the Histadrut elections in May, Mapai maintained its strength, with 57.7% of the votes, as against 14.6% for Aḥdut ha-Avodah and 12.5% for Mapam. Ben-Gurion resumed his place at the head of Mapai's list of candidates for the forthcoming parliamentary elections and it was assumed that he would return to the premiership.

In the tense political atmosphere, the outcome of the Kasztner trial became a prominent issue. An immigrant from Hungary, Malkiel Gruenwald, had been prosecuted by the state on a charge of libeling Rudolf (Israel) Kasztner, a government official and a Mapai candidate for the Knesset. Gruenwald had charged Kasztner with collaborating with the Nazis as a leader of Hungarian Jewry during the war. The court awarded nominal damages against Gruenwald, in effect confirming his charges. Judge Benjamin Halevi declared that Kasztner had "sold his soul to Satan" in Hungary by concealing the truth from the Jews in return for the Nazis' agreement to allow a trainload of privileged individuals, including Kasztner's relatives and friends, to leave the country. When the attorney general announced his intention to appeal, Herut submitted a motion of no confidence in the government, and the General Zionist ministers abstained on the vote. Sharett thereupon submitted his resignation and on June 28 re-formed the cabinet without them.

The Third Knesset—1955-59. At the general election which took place on July 26, 1955, at the end of the four-year term of the Second Knesset, Mapai lost votes to the left-wing labor parties, while the middle class electors, apparently disappointed with the General Zionists' performance in office, again turned to Herut, which became the leading opposition party (see Table p. 116-7). At the municipal elections, which took place simultaneously, many electors distinguished between national and local issues: Abba Khoushi (Mapai) was reelected as mayor of Haifa with an increased majority, and Gershon Agron, of the same party, became mayor of Jerusalem.

After negotiations lasting three months, Ben-Gurion succeeded in bringing the left-wing labor parties into his Cabinet, which was approved by the Knesset on November 2 by 78 votes to 32. There were nine Mapai ministers: Ben-Gurion as prime minister and minister of defense; Sharett, Eshkol, Golda Myerson (Meir), and Shitrit in the same posts: Pinḥas Sapir as minister of commerce and industry; Zalman Aranne as minister of education and culture; Kaddish Luz as minister of agriculture; and Perez Naftali as minister without portfolio. Shapira and Burg of the National Religious Party (formed in 1956 by the union of Mizrachi and Ha-Po'el ha-Mizrachi), retained their former posts. Two Aḥdut ha-Avodah representatives, Israel Bar-Yehudah and Moshe Carmel, became ministers of the interior and of transport, while Mordekhai Bentov and Israel Barzilai, of Mapam became ministers of development and health respectively. Pinḥas Rosen (Progressives) returned to the ministry of justice.

In his speech during the debate on the program of the new government, Ben-Gurion emphasized the gravity of the security situation. The threat of imminent war hung over political life during the months that followed. The atmosphere in the Knesset grew more and more heated, with frequent vociferous clashes, mostly of a personal character, between Ben-Gurion and Begin. In the light of growing disagreements with Moshe Sharett over the coordination of defense and foreign policy, Ben-Gurion decided that a change must be made in the Foreign Ministry, and the Mapai Central Council reluctantly approved Sharett's resignation by 35 votes to 7, with 74 abstentions. Golda Meir took over as foreign minister, while Mordekhai Namir succeeded her in the Ministry of Labor. On June 28, 1956, Pinḥas Lavon returned to public life as secretary general of the Histadrut in succession to Namir.

Israel's victory in the Sinai Campaign brought Ben-Gurion to the pinnacle of his popularity. Mapam, though disapproving the operation, remained in the Cabinet, while Ḥerut granted the premier unwonted praise. However, the step-by-step withdrawal, first from Sinai and then from the Gaza Strip and Sharm el-Sheikh, put an end to the political truce, Ḥerut accusing the government of squandering the gains achieved by the army's victories.

A cabinet crisis arose in May 1957 over the question of adhesion to the Eisenhower Doctrine, which empowered the U.S. President to assist any country threatened with communist aggression. Aḥdut ha-Avodah and Mapam argued that adhesion might embroil Israel in the cold war and worsen the chances of Jews being allowed to leave the Soviet Union. However, when Ben-Gurion made a statement in the Knesset in support of adhesion, on June 3, Aḥdut ha-Avodah and Mapam were prevailed upon to abstain instead of voting against the government. Ḥerut and the General Zionists also abstained, mainly on the ground that the statement did not go far enough.

On October 28, 1957, President Ben-Zvi was nominated for a second term by ten of the parties and reelected by 76 votes, with Ḥerut, the Communists, and Agudat Israel abstaining.

Another cabinet crisis broke out in December 1957 in connection with relations with Germany. It became known that "an important personality" (later identified as Chief of Staff Moshe Dayan) was to go to Germany to discuss the acquisition of certain types of armaments. Under pressure from the left-wing parties, the plan was canceled. Ben-Gurion accused the Aḥdut ha-Avodah ministers of leaking the information to the press, and demanded their resignation. When the ministers refused, Ben-Gurion submitted the government's resignation on December 31. The crisis was resolved after the left-wing parties agreed that coalition ministers and their parties must vote for government motions in the Knesset, and solemnly undertook to maintain Cabinet secrecy. Ben-Gurion then re-formed his government, which was approved in the Knesset on Jan. 7, 1958.

On February 12, the Knesset adopted the first of the basic laws which were to form Israel's constitution—the law dealing with the Knesset itself. A General Zionist proposal to institute an electoral system containing elements of both proportional and constituency representation was rejected. Mapai, which saw no prospect of obtaining a majority for the constituency system, proposed that the law should not specify the method of election, but this motion was also rejected. An important clause in the law, as finally adopted, provided that no amendment to the electoral system could be adopted without the support of 61 of the 120 Knesset members.

A third Cabinet crisis, this time involving the National Religious Party, arose over the regulations issued by Minister of Interior Israel Bar-Yehudah to define a Jew for the purposes of the population register, that were not based on religious law. When the regulations were approved by the Knesset, the two N.R.P. ministers resigned on June 29. On December 3 the Knesset approved the appointment of Rabbi Ya'akov Moshe Toledano (nonparty), Sephardi chief rabbi of Tel Aviv, as minister of religious affairs— the first time this portfolio had been taken out of the hands of the N.R.P.

The death of Yosef Sprinzak, the first speaker of the Knesset, in January 1958, was followed by a minor revolt against what was regarded as Mapai's monopoly of the major offices in the state. On March 3, 1959, two of the coalition parties joined the opposition in electing as his successor the senior deputy speaker, Nahum Nir (Aḥdut ha-Avodah) by 53 votes against 41 for the Mapai candidate, Berl Locker, after Sharett, who had been offered general support, refused to stand.

Toward the end of June, a Cabinet crisis broke out over the sale of Israel arms to West Germany. Ben-Gurion claimed that the transaction was necessary in order to ensure German support for Israel and that it had been approved by the government. This was denied by the Mapam and Aḥdut ha-Avodah ministers, who voted against a motion expressly approving the transaction. Ben-Gurion thereupon demanded the resignation of the ministers voting with the opposition, and, when they refused, submitted his resignation on July 5. The General Zionists and the N.R.P. refused to join a new government under Ben-Gurion, and the president announced that the existing cabinet would have to remain in office until a new one could be formed after the forthcoming elections.

During the month of July the election campaign was overshadowed by a series of riots by new immigrants in the Wadi Salib quarter of Haifa, in the new town of Migdal ha-Emek, and in Beersheba, which threatened to exacerbate relations between immigrants from Muslim countries, who complained of discrimination and hardship, and the more settled sections of the community consisting mostly of Ashkenazim. Mapai introduced new blood into its list of candidates, notably Moshe Dayan, Abba Eban, who had recently returned to Israel after eight years as ambassador to the U.S. and the UN, Giora Josephtal, treasurer of the Jewish Agency, and Shimon Peres, director general of the Defense Ministry—all regarded as protégés of Ben-Gurion.

The Fourth Knesset—1959-61. The elections to the Fourth Knesset, which were held on Nov. 3, 1959, gave Mapai the greatest victory of its history. Since the Sinai Campaign, the country had been enjoying a rapid rise in the standard of living. Border incidents had almost completely ceased on the southern frontiers and were infrequent in the north and east. The port of Eilat was developing, and new friendships were being forged with Asian and African countries. Apparently the Wadi Salib riots and the emergence of an intransigent movement claiming to represent the oriental communities led many electors to rally round the largest party, which promised to guarantee stable government. The electorate responded to Mapai's campaign slogan, *"Haggidu ken la-zaken"*—"Say Yes to the Old Man"—and none of the "ethnic" lists representing non-Ashkenazi communities won a place.

Mapai gained seven seats, while the General Zionists lost five, Aḥdut ha-Avodah three, and the Communists three. Ḥerut gained two seats, consolidating its position as the leading opposition party. In the new cabinet, which was approved on December 18, there were three new Mapai ministers: Eban, without portfolio; Dayan, agriculture; and Josephtal, labor (replacing Namir, who became mayor of Tel Aviv). Shapira and Burg, of the N.R.P., rejoined the Cabinet as ministers of the interior and social welfare respectively, on the understanding that the registration problem (see above) would be solved to their satisfaction, but with the religious affairs portfolio in the hands of Rabbi Toledano. Yizḥak Ben-Aharon of Aḥdut ha-Avodah became minister of transport, and Peres deputy minister of defense. Mordekhai Ish-Shalom succeeded Gershon Agron, who had died a few days before the elections, as mayor of Jerusalem.

One of the new government's first tasks was to arrange for the election of the chief rabbis. The term of office of the Sephardi incumbent, Rabbi Isaac Nissim, was due to expire on Feb. 21, 1960, and the post of Ashkenazi chief rabbi had been vacant since the death of Rabbi Isaac Halevi Herzog on July 25, 1959. A section of the Sephardi community, supported by Rabbi Toledano, opposed the reelection of Chief Rabbi Nissim, while the Ashkenazi post was contested by Rabbi Isser Unterman, supported by the N.R.P., and Rabbi Shelomo Goren, chief chaplain of the Israel Defense Forces, who was backed by the prime minister and Mapai. Prolonged controversy over the organization of the elections resulted in their repeated postponement until March 15, 1964, when rabbis Nissim and Unterman were elected.

A lengthy dispute over the claims of the secondary teachers for salary increases and recognition of their separate union led to the resignation, on April 24, 1960, of Zalman Aranne, minister of education and culture. The portfolio, temporarily held by the prime minister, was entrusted to Abba Eban on August 3. Another change in the Cabinet was the appointment of Binyamin Minz (Po'alei Agudat Israel) as minister of posts, on July 18. This appointment was followed by vehement protests and public demonstrations by Agudat Israel and ultra-Orthodox circles against what they regarded as a betrayal of the united Agudah front.

Toward the end of 1960, Israel's political life was convulsed by the aftermath of the events that had surrounded Lavon's resignation in 1954. At a trial for a criminal offense, in August 1960, a former witness at the Olshan-Dori inquiry testified that two officers, one still serving in the army, had suborned him in 1954 to give false testimony against Lavon. A committee headed by Supreme Court Justice Haim Cohn was appointed, on Ben-Gurion's orders, to inquire into the allegation against the officer still in service. Informed of the new development, Lavon demanded that Ben-Gurion publicly clear him of responsibility for the 1954 operation. Ben-Gurion, replying that he had no authority to do so, asked Lavon to await the result of the inquiry, but Lavon insisted on putting his case to the Foreign Affairs and Security Committee of the Knesset.

In his evidence before the committee, Lavon accused Shimon Peres, who had been director general of the Ministry of Defense, of disloyal behavior in the course of the Olshan-Dori inquiry, and alleged that unnamed officials of the ministry were conducting a press campaign against him. It transpired that there had also been tension between Lavon and Dayan. The proceedings at the committee's sessions, which are always kept secret, were published almost verbatim in the press every day, and a violent public controversy ensued, which the opposition utilized to discredit Ben-Gurion and Mapai.

The Cohn committee report, published in part on October 23, endorsed the charge of subornation of perjury, and the officer concerned resigned from the army. Sharett stated that if at the time he had been aware of the evidence now disclosed, he would not have accepted Lavon's resignation, and Lavon declared himself satisfied with this statement as clearing his name. However, Ben-Gurion maintained that only a judicial inquiry could decide whether Lavon or the officer had given the order for the 1954 intelligence operation, and the controversy continued.

On October 30, an all-party Cabinet committee of seven, headed by Minister of Justice Pinḥas Rosen, was set up to consider what further action, if any, was necessary. The committee, which examined the documents but did not interrogate witnesses, declared itself satisfied that Lavon had not given the order, and recommended that the matter be regarded as closed. The report was endorsed by the Cabinet on December 25, but Ben-Gurion declared that it had overstepped its terms of reference. He denounced its findings as a "miscarriage of justice," again demanded a judicial inquiry, and announced that he was taking a vacation of indefinite duration.

On January 12, 1961, he bitterly attacked Lavon for conducting "a poisonous war" of "backbiting and slander." On January 30 the Knesset rejected a motion of no confidence in the government by 77 votes to 26; but in the debate, however, the Mapam, Aḥdut ha-Avodah, and Progressive representatives severely criticized Ben-Gurion's attitude, and he submitted his resignation on the following day. He asserted that the Cabinet committee's findings were "incompatible with the fundamental principles of justice," since it had implicitly condemned the officer without giving him a hearing.

On February 4 the Mapai Central Council decided by 159 votes to 96 to remove Lavon from his office as Histadrut secretary-general. Although Lavon's behavior during the controversy was offered as the reason for his dismissal, it was widely assumed that most members were deferring to Ben-Gurion's animosity against Lavon. President Ben-Zvi called on Ben-Gurion to form a new Cabinet, but Mapam, Aḥdut ha-Avodah, and the Progressives were not prepared to serve under him, while the N.R.P. was unwilling to be Mapai's only ally in the Cabinet. Since Mapai refused to put forward a new candidate for the premiership, the deadlock was complete, and on March 13 the Knesset decided that general elections should be held on August 15, 1961.

The Fifth Knesset—1961–65. Mapai decided to take no official stand on the Lavon Affair and ignored it during the election campaign, but all the other parties and some academics denounced Ben-Gurion's behavior as a danger to democracy. Mapai lost five seats and its affiliated Arab 127 parties one. The new Liberal Party, which had been formed by the merger of the General Zionists and the Progressives on April 25, gained three seats, totaling 17 and equaling Ḥerut.

The negotiations for a new government, conducted by Levi Eshkol on behalf of Ben-Gurion, were prolonged and difficult. At first, Mapam, Aḥdut ha-Avodah, the N.R.P., and the Liberals combined as the "Club of Four" to insist that Mapai, with its reduced strength, should no longer have a majority in the cabinet. Ultimately, Eshkol induced Aḥdut ha-Avodah to join the coalition without Mapam. In the new Cabinet, which was approved in the Knesset on November 2 by 63 votes to 46, Mapai had 11 ministers, the N.R.P. three, and Aḥdut ha-Avodah two. Po'alei Agudat Israel also supported the coalition and was represented by a deputy minister. The new Mapai ministers were: Dov Joseph, Justice; Eliyahu Sasson, Posts; and Yosef Almogi, without portfolio. Josephtal became minister of housing and development. (He died in office on August 22, 1962, and was succeeded by Almogi.) Aḥdut ha-Avodah was represented by Yigal Allon, Labor, and Yiẓhak Ben-Aharon, Transport. Ḥayyim Moshe Shapira took over the portfolios of Health and Interior, while a third N.R.P. member, Zerah Warhaftig, joined the Cabinet as minister of religious affairs. Ben-Aharon, resigning on May 28, 1962, because of differences of opinion with his colleagues in Aḥdut ha-Avodah over a rapprochement with Mapai, was replaced by Israel Bar-Yehudah of the same party. On January 11, 1963, Ben-Aharon published a long article in the dailies *Davar* and *La-Merḥav* calling for a union (*hitaḥadut*) of Socialist workers in Israel, centered on the three workers' parties and the religious workers, on the basis of an agreed plan of action. The proposal, largely realized in 1968 after the Six-Day War, was rejected at the time by Mapam, coolly received by Aḥdut ha-Avodah, and cautiously welcomed by Mapai.

During this period there was considerable controversy over military government in areas inhabited mainly by

Arabs. Although restrictions had been gradually relaxed since the founding of the state, demands for abolishing military government were pressed by Herut, the Liberals, and the left-wing labor parties, at times with N.R.P. support. These proposals were defeated by narrow majorities only: 4 votes in 1962 and 1 vote in 1963.

President Ben-Zvi, who died on April 23, 1963, was succeeded on May 21 by Zalman Shazar, who received 67 votes on the first ballot to 33 for Perez Bernstein, with seven abstentions.

On June 16, 1963, Ben-Gurion submitted his resignation "because of personal needs, unconnected with any state problems or any particular event." Before resigning, he had received a report on the Lavon Affair, which he had commissioned from a journalist who had been given full access to all the papers. The conclusions of the report, if accepted, would have undermined those of the 1960 Cabinet committee headed by Pinhas Rosen. On Ben-Gurion's recommendation, Levi Eshkol was nominated by Mapai as his successor, and completed the negotiations for the formation of a new cabinet in one week, receiving a vote of confidence from the Knesset on June 26. Sapir became minister of finance, as well as commerce and industry, Aranne returned to the Ministry of Education and Culture, and Eban became deputy prime minister. Eshkol described his cabinet as "a government of continuity," but there were signs of conflict between the new men sponsored by Ben-Gurion and the old guard of Mapai. Dayan at first declined to reenter the cabinet, and its composition was regarded as reflecting a victory for the veterans.

Eshkol adopted a more conciliatory tone than his predecessor, both in his reaction to opposition criticism and in foreign affairs, especially in references to the Soviet Union. After a time, however, he was plagued by dissension within his own party, on the one hand from a group called Min ha-Yesod ("From the Foundations"), formed primarily by supporters of Lavon, and, on the other, from Ben-Gurion and his supporters. Ben-Gurion, who remained a member 129 of the Knesset, accused Eshkol of weakness in foreign policy and of bypassing party institutions in order to conciliate the Min ha-Yesod group.

On October 22, 1964, Ben-Gurion submitted a dossier containing an account of the Lavon Affair to the minister of justice, Dov Joseph, and the attorney general, along with an analysis by two lawyers of the proceedings and conclusions of the 1960 Cabinet committee, and demanded a judicial inquiry into the committee's work. Joseph reported to the Cabinet on Ben-Gurion's dossier on December 6, severely criticizing the work of the 1960 Cabinet committee, mainly for not having interrogated witnesses, including the senior officer involved. While rejecting the demand for an inquiry into its proceedings, he proposed a comprehensive official inquiry into the 1954 Lavon Affair. Eshkol rejected the proposal and, when he met with strong minority opposition in the Mapai Central Council, submitted his resignation, demanding that the cabinet have unfettered discretion to decide the matter without party interference. Mapai unanimously called upon him to re-form his Cabinet, which he presented to the Knesset, unchanged, on December 23. On November 6 Moshe Dayan resigned from the Cabinet because of "the absence of identity of views which a minister must have with the prime minister" and was replaced by Ḥayyim Gvati. On November 15 the Mapai Central Council approved an agreement between Eshkol and Israel Galili, the leader of Aḥdut ha-Avodah, on the establishment of an Alignment (Ma'arakh) between the two parties, which would submit joint lists of candidates at all elections and act as one body in the Knesset. Ben-Gurion and his supporters objected to two provisions in the agreement: the pigeonholing until the end of the Sixth Knesset of Mapai's demand for electoral reform, and the maintenance by Aḥdut ha-Avodah of a separate faction in the Histadrut.

The clash between Eshkol's and Ben-Gurion's supporters came to a head at the Mapai Convention of February 16–18, 1965. Fifty-nine percent of the delegates refused to support Ben-Gurion's attitude on the Lavon Affair, and the Alignment was approved by 63%. The rift deepened. Ben-Gurion continued to attack Eshkol, accusing him of having been mainly responsible for the 1960 Cabinet committee's decision. Eshkol called upon those members of the administration who shared Ben-Gurion's opinion of him to "release themselves and me from working together," and Almogi and Peres submitted their resignations. Ḥayyim Zadok joined the cabinet on May 23 as minister of commerce and industry, and, after the death of Israel Bar-Yehudah, Moshe Carmel took over transport.

On May 20, the day after the signature of the agreement setting up the Alignment, Ben-Gurion declared that, despite his appreciation of Eshkol's work in the past, he had come to the conclusion that Eshkol lacked traits essential to the responsible post of prime minister of Israel. On June 3, the Mapai Central Council confirmed Eshkol's candidacy for premiership at the forthcoming elections by 179 to 103.

On June 29 Ben-Gurion announced that he intended to submit an independent list for the elections and, on July 14 seven Mapai members of the Knesset seceded to form a new faction, Rafi (Reshimat Po'alei Yisrael; "Israel Labor List"), which was led by Ben-Gurion, Peres and Almogi, later joined by Dayan. After an acrimonious trial before a party court, the Rafi supporters were expelled from Mapai.

Meanwhile, on April 26, the Liberal Party combined with Herut to form the Herut-Liberal Bloc, called Gaḥal (Gush Ḥerut-Liberalim), whereupon seven former Progressives broke away to form the Independent Liberal Party. In August the Communist Party split into the New Communist List, called Rakaḥ (Reshimah Komunistit Ḥadashah), which was mainly Arab, and the Israel Communist Party, Maki (Miflagah Komunistit Yisre'elit), which was mainly Jewish.

At the Histadrut elections on September 19, the Alignment list won 50.1% of the votes, of which Aḥdut ha-Avodah received 17% and Mapai 34%, placing it for the first time in its history in a minority. Gaḥal, contesting for

131

Polling committee convened for instruction before the 1965 general elections. Courtesy Government Press Office, Tel Aviv.

the first time, obtained 15.3%, Mapam 14.5%, and Rafi 12.1%.

The Sixth Knesset—1965–69. In the election campaign, Eshkol was supported by a nonparty Citizens for Eshkol movement. At the polls which were held on November 2, 1965, the Alignment won 45 seats, four more than the combined pre-election strength of its constituents, while Rafi, with 10, gained two. Gaḥal, with 26, lost one, as did the N.R.P. and Mapam. The Independent Liberals, with 5 seats, lost 2 and Maki lost 3 seats to Rakaḥ, while Uri

Avneri, the editor of a popular weekly, *Ha-Olam ha-Zeh,* was returned on an independent list. In the Jerusalem municipal elections, Teddy Kollek, of Rafi, scored a personal success and was elected mayor with the support of Gaḥal and the religious parties.

Eshkol's new cabinet, which received a vote of confidence by 71 votes to 41 on January 12, 1966, was marked by the inclusion of Mapam, represented by Mordekhai Bentov, Housing, and Israel Barzilai, Health. Abba Eban replaced Golda Meir as foreign minister, while Joseph was dropped and replaced by Ya'akov Shimshon Shapiro as minister of justice. Israel Galili (Aḥdut ha-Avodah) became minister without portfolio (later taking over responsibility for information); and Moshe Kol (Independent Liberal) minister of development and of tourism. Ḥayyim Zadok resigned in November over differences of opinion with the finance minister, and was succeeded as minister of commerce and industry by Ze'ev Sharef. Behor Shitrit, minister of police, resigned as of November 21, and was succeeded by Eliyahu Sasson, the minister of posts, whose portfolio was taken over by Israel Yeshayahu (Alignment), the first minister of Yemenite extraction.

In the Knesset debates, Rafi joined Gaḥal in opposition criticizing severely the government's economic slowdown policy and accusing Eshkol and Eban of unrealistic optimism in foreign and security affairs. However, Rafi supported the government's decision, denounced by Ḥerut, to accept West-Germany's offer to establish diplomatic relations (March 1966), although Ben-Gurion severely criticized the handling of the negotiations on German economic aid to Israel the following year. Three Ḥerut members, headed by Shemuel Tamir, seceded early in 1967 and formed the Free Center faction, joined the following year by a Liberal member.

The threat posed by Egyptian troop concentrations in Sinai in May 1967 led to a widespread demand for the establishment of a Cabinet of national unity. Menahem Begin, of Ḥerut, proposed that Ben-Gurion return to the 133

Meeting at which the Mapai, Aḥdut ha-Avodah and Rafi parties merged, January 1968. Seen left to right: Israel Galili, Levi Eshkol, Yizḥak Tabenkin, Shimon Peres, and Zalman Aranne. Courtesy Government Press Office, Tel Aviv.

premiership to strengthen public confidence, or, alternatively, that the defense portfolio be taken over by Moshe Dayan. Eshkol proposed appointing Yigal Allon as defense minister, but Dayan's candidacy was strongly supported by the National Religious Party and a large section of Mapai. Eshkol gave way and the government decided to co-opt Dayan as minister of defense, along with Begin and Yosef Saphir (Liberal) as ministers without portfolio. These appointments were confirmed by the Knesset on June 5.

During the negotiations on the enlargement of the cabinet, Shimon Peres, on behalf of Rafi, offered to reunite with Mapai and, after the Six-Day War, Mapai opened negotiations on unification with Rafi and Aḥdut ha-Avodah. The result of these discussions was the establishment of the united Israel Labor Party on Jan. 21, 1968, despite Ben-Gurion's opposition. The governing bodies of the new party were nominated by the partners: 57% by Mapai and 21½% each by Aḥdut ha-Avodah and Rafi. Golda Meir was elected secretary-general, with Shimon Peres (Rafi) and Avraham Gevelber (Aḥdut ha-Avodah) as deputies. At this stage the party was, in effect, a federation of three factions and, while there was harmonious cooperation between Mapai and Aḥdut ha-Avodah, the "ex-Rafi" faction was restive. Its demand for the holding of an elected conference before the imminent Histadrut and Knesset polls was turned down and the struggle for power between supporters of the veteran leadership, whose candidate for the ultimate succession was Allon, and those of Dayan, whose growing popularity was attested by mass petitions and public opinion polls, continued. The appointment of Allon, on July 2, as deputy prime minister and minister of immigrant absorption was interpreted by some sections of the public as meant to enhance his prestige, and the cooption of Yosef Almogi, who had supported Rafi, to succeed Allon as minister of labor as an attempt to neutralize a leading member of the disaffected faction. Pinḥas Sapir, also regarded as a possible candidate for the premiership, now entered the party arena. Golda Meir resigned as secretary-general and Sapir was elected on Aug. 2 to succeed her, remaining in the Cabinet as minister without portfolio, while Ze'ev Sharef took over finance in addition to commerce and industry.

Despite Rafi opposition, a new alliance, or alignment, was concluded between the Israel Labor Party and Mapam on Jan. 20, 1969. It held 63 seats in the Knesset (67 together with the affiliated Arab lists)—the first time any party or bloc had commanded an absolute majority. Questions of policy in the 'West Bank' and the Gaza Strip, under Israel military administration as a result of the Six-Day War had come to the fore. Sapir criticized Dayan's policy of integrating the areas in the Israel economy and warned against the danger of incorporating a million Arabs in Israel. At conferences of the Rafi faction there was strong support for the proposal to break up the union and fight the elections independently under the leadership of Dayan, who, it was hoped, would win widespread popular support.

Meanwhile, the sudden death of Levi Eshkol on Feb. 26, 1969, threatened to precipitate the struggle for the succession, but the party quickly rallied round the candidacy of Golda Meir. On March 7 its central council unanimously nominated her to succeed Eshkol and on the 17th a new national unity Cabinet, with her as prime minister, was installed. It was identical in composition with the old one, except for the change in the premiership, and was based on the same policies, only the foreign affairs and security chapter being redrafted in agreement with Gaḥal. Dayan's attitude to his political future remained equivocal for a time. He expressed uneasiness at the alliance with Mapam and did not commit himself to the Alignment ticket until it was agreed that the ex-Rafi faction should nominate its own candidates to the Knesset and the post-election cabinet, and the Labor Party convention, held on August 3 5, empowered its spokesmen, if they wished, to advocate territorial claims constituting what he called "the new map of Israel." A number of ex-members of Rafi, led by Ben-Gurion, formed the independent National List ("Reshimah Mamlakhtit") to fight the elections.

The Histadrut elections, held on September 2, were contested by all the parties, except the religious ones; there was also a Religious Workers' List (Ha-Oved ha-Dati), associated with Labor. The result was a setback for the Alignment, which obtained 62.11% of a considerably reduced poll (in addition to 3.85 for the National List and 3.06 for Ha-Oved ha-Dati), while gains were made by Gaḥal and the Independent Liberals.

The Seventh Knesset, 1969–73. The parliamentary election campaign for the Seventh Knesset was comparatively subdued. Under a law passed in February 1969 (subsequently amended to conform to a Supreme Court ruling), election expenditures were subsidized by the state in proportion to party strengths in the outgoing Knesset, new lists benefiting on condition that they succeeded in electing at least one member.

At the elections which were held on Oct. 28, the Labor-Mapam Alignment lost its overall majority, dropping from 63 seats to 56 but commanding 50% of the seats (60) together with the Druze and Arab members allied with it. Gaḥal, with 26, regained the seats it had lost to the Free Center, which were reduced to 2. The National List obtained 4 places; the National Religious Party, with 12 seats, and Ha-Olam ha-Zeh, with 2, gained one each, and the Independent Liberals, with 4, lost one. In the negotiations for the new Cabinet, Gaḥal demanded representation in proportion to its Knesset strength and agreement on a new statement of basic principles. Mapam refused to enter into

Ḥerut Central Committee meeting held to choose half of the six Gaḥal ministers in the National Coalition Government, Tel Aviv, December 1969. In the center, wearing glasses, is Menahem Begin. Courtesy Government Press Office, Tel Aviv.

full partnership with Gaḥal, and its representatives joined the government only as ministers without portfolio and with limited responsibility.

The new Cabinet had 24 members: 12 Labor, 6 Gaḥal, 3 N.R.P., 2 Mapam and one Independent Liberal. There was no change in the premiership, defense and foreign affairs. Pinḥas Sapir returned to the ministry of finance; Allon, who remained deputy prime minister, took over Education.

There were ministers without portfolio: Begin, Galili, Peres (who was given special responsibility for development in the administered areas), Aryeh L. Dultzin (Liberal), and Israel Barzilai and Victor Shemtov (Mapam). Other posts were unchanged. Mapam refused to take up the portfolios offered to them, Health and Immigrant Absorption, in view of the admission of Gaḥal as full coalition partners.

In the late summer Mapam decided, in view of the government's readiness to consider a more flexible attitude to the question of a possible settlement with the Arabs, to accept full cabinet responsibility; on July 27 Victor Shemtov became minister of health and Natan Peled joined the Cabinet in place of Israel Barzilai, recently deceased, as minister of immigrant absorption. The government's decision to accept the American peace initiative led to the break-up of the National Unity Cabinet by the resignation, with effect from August 6, of the six Gaḥal ministers, though most of Gaḥal's Liberal wing, while opposing the government's decision, were against resigning. Peres took over the ministries of Transport and Posts (the name of the latter was changed, on his proposal, to Communications), Sapir became minister of commerce and industry as well as of finance, and Gvati assumed responsibility for Development, in addition to Agriculture. Gaḥal's return to opposition helped to enliven the proceedings of the Knesset and political life in general. The government's declared readiness to contemplate withdrawal from part of the occupied territories in the event of a peace settlement was also opposed by a considerable section of the National Religious Party and by a non-party anti-withdrawal movement.

The general relaxation of military tension and the cessation of almost daily military and civilian casualties were accompanied by a rise in domestic tension, as problems that had taken second place to the defense effort rose to the surface, although defense costs were still high, accounting for one-third of the state budget and one-quarter of the GNP. The economic boom, the influx of foreign capital, the shortage of labor and the resulting wage claims led to inflationary pressures and rising prices. Rapid expansion of economic activity led to larger incomes in the higher brackets, some conspicuous consumption of luxuries, and a considerable measure of inequality in living standards.

These phenomena aroused discontent among the lower-income strata, and there were spasmodic demonstrations and riots by a group of young men, mostly school dropouts and juvenile delinquents from oriental immigrant families still living in slum conditions, who adopted the name "Black Panthers." The rise in the marriage rate, the boom conditions, the higher standards of living, and the increased immigration pushed up the demand for housing and, consequently, the cost of accommodation. Young couples demanded more government housing aid and some of them resented the provision of comparatively spacious dwellings for immigrants immediately on arrival.

The Government attempted to meet social needs. While the State budget grew from IL 11 billion in 1970/71 to IL 15.9 billion in 1972/73, the allocation for defense went up slightly from IL 4.8 billion to IL 5.2 billion, but the budget for education was increased from IL 644 million to IL 1,074 million, for housing from IL 671 million to IL 884 million, and for social welfare from IL 70 million to IL 113 million, while the allocations for social services went up still further in the budget for 1973/74. The number of dwellings completed by public and private builders rose from 25,630 in 1969 to 47,500 in 1972 and dwellings started from 36,940 to 62,530 in the same period.

Economic problems, particularly that of inflation, also came to the fore. The wage restraint of 1971 was followed in 1972 by a spate of claims over and above a moderate general wage increase agreed upon between the Histadrut and the employers' associations, followed by frequent strikes, especially in the public services. Prices rose by about 12% in 1972 and at the end of the year economists warned of inflationary dangers ahead. As election year approached, economic and social questions played a prominent part, side by side with the nature of Israel's peace policies and the question of the future borders, in the maneuverings of the political parties in preparation for the polls in October 1973.

There was heated controversy over several issues connected with religion.

A Cabinet crisis loomed over a proposal to institute civil marriage for those disqualified from marriage by the Rabbinate, such as *mamzerim* and *kohanim* wishing to marry divorcées. Much of the support for the proposal was due to the case of a brother and sister who had been adjudged as *mamzerim*, because their mother had remarried without obtaining a valid Jewish divorce. When Gideon Hausner, of the Independent Liberal Party, introduced a bill to provide for civil marriage for religiously disqualified couples, Prime Minister Golda Meir stated that the proposal violated the clause in the coalition agreement providing for the maintenance of the status quo in matters of religion. A serious crisis was narrowly averted when the vote on the bill, which was debated by the Knesset on July 6, 1972, was postponed.

The Labor-Mapam Alignment's other Coalition partner, the National Religious Party, was affected by a bill proposed by Shelomo Lorincz (Agudat Israel) to amend the Law of Return (Amendment No. 2), which defined a Jew for the purposes of the law as someone born of a Jewish mother or converted to Judaism. The Lorincz bill proposed adding to the word *giyyur*—"conversion"—the word *ka-din*—"according to [halakhic] law." A strong section of the NRP felt that its Knesset representatives must vote for the bill, even at the cost of violating coalition discipline, but it was decided by a majority to abstain.

The prime minister and most Labor members hoped that at least some of the problems with which the Hausner bill was meant to deal could be solved by a more liberal interpretation of the *halakhah* in specific cases. They attached great importance, therefore, to the forthcoming elections to the Chief Rabbinate, in which, they hoped, Rabbi S. Goren, chief rabbi of Tel Aviv and former chief rabbi of the Israel army, who was supported by the NRP as well as by the Labor-Mapam Alignment, would succeed Chief Rabbi Issar Yehuda Unterman. The elections ultimately took place on Oct. 15. Rabbi Goren was elected by 89 votes to 57 for Rabbi Unterman and Rabbi Ovadiah Yosef was elected Sephardi Chief Rabbi by 81 votes to 68 votes for the incumbent, Rabbi Isaac Nissim.

One of the first problems with which Chief Rabbi Goren dealt was that of the Langer brother and sister, on which he had previously written a detailed halakhic opinion. On Nov. 19 he announced that he and eight *dayyanim* had ruled that the Langers were not *mamzerim*, and they were married to their respective bethrothed on the same day. The decision was widely welcomed and the ILP acceded to Chief Rabbi Goren's request to postpone the vote on the Hausner bill for a year in order to give him the opportunity to find halakhic solutions to some of the pressing problems, but it was bitterly denounced by Agudat Israel and more extreme Orthodox circles.

The Israel Labor Party held its first elected convention in April, 1971. The elections were held on a personal basis, but it was estimated that the ex-Mapai faction had increased its strength at the expense of ex-Rafi.

A debate was held in the Labor Party Secretariat toward the end of 1972 on the policies to be followed in the administered areas. Despite the intention to restrict the discussion to practical and immediate questions, such as the relations between the two economies and the social problems involved in the large-scale employment 141 of Arab labor in Israel, most of the speakers expressed their views on the possibility of peace negotiations with Jordan and the future status of the territories. In several public speeches, Defense Minister Moshe Dayan had stated that there was no prospect of a peace settlement with Jordan in the near future and that, during an interim period which he estimated at 10–15 years, the Arabs of the administered territories would continue to be under Israel rule while bearing Jordanian citizenship. He also called for more extensive Israel settlement in the areas. In the debate in the Labor Party Secretariat, Finance Minister Pinhas Sapir, Deputy Prime Minister Yigal Allon, Foreign Minister Abba Eban, Commerce and Industry Minister Haim Bar-Lev and others stressed the demographic and other dangers involved in the inclusion of a million Arabs from Judea, Samaria, and the Gaza Strip in Israel. With varying degrees of emphasis, they envisaged a peace settlement in which most of Judea and Samaria (and, according to a few, the Gaza Strip) would be united with Jordan, although no Jordanian troops would be allowed to cross the Jordan River westward and, according to the Allon Plan, there would be a protective belt of Israeli settlements along the Jordan Valley. Other speakers declared that, in any case, Jordan was not prepared to make territorial concessions for the sake of peace and objected to talk of an Israeli withdrawal.

Gahal (the Herut-Liberal Bloc), especially Menahem Begin and Ezer Weizman, the leaders of the Herut wing, continued to advocate the integrity of the entire Land of Israel (in practice, the area west of the River Jordan and the Golan Heights) and opposed withdrawal from any part of the areas which would involve the renewed partition of Erez Israel. They also opposed any withdrawal of Israel troops from the Suez Canal as part of an interim or partial settlement with Egypt.

In the National Religious Party, opinion was also hardening against the idea of withdrawal from any part of the historic Land of Israel. Mapam opposed any settlement

Results of Knesset Elections (1969 and 1973)

Party	Seventh Knesset Oct. 28, 1969		Eighth Knesset Dec. 31, 1973	
Electorate	1,748,710		2,037,478	
Valid votes cast	1,367,743		1,566,855	
	%	Seats	%	Seats
Labor-Mapam Alignment[1]	46.2	56	39.8	51
Arabs (associated with Alignment)	3.6	4[2]	3.1	3[3]
Gaḥal (Herut-Liberal Bloc)	21.7	26	—	—
National (*Mamlakhti*) List	3.1	4[4]	—	—
Free Center	1.2	2	—	—
Likkud (incl. Gaḥal, National List, Free Center, etc.)	—	—	30.1	39
Independent Liberals	3.2	4	3.6	4
Civil Rights Movement	—	—	2.2	3
National Religious Party	9.7	12[5]	8.3	10
Torah Religious Front (Agudat Israel and Po'alei Agudat Israel)	5.0	6	3.9	5
Rakaḥ (New Communist List)	2.8	3	3.4	4
Maki (Israel Communist Party)	1.1	1	—	—
Moked (Communists and New Left)	—	—	1.4	1
Others	3.3	2[6]	4.2	—

Israel Labor Party (merger of Mapai, Aḥduṭ ha-Avodah and Rafi) and Mapam.

Cooperation and Fraternity (2) and Progress and Development (2).

Progress and Development (2) and Bedouin and Villagers (1).

Cooperation and Fraternity did not win a seat.

One member left the party during the term of the Seventh Knesset and joined the Alignment.

One member left during the term of the Seventh Knesset and sat as an independent member. At the 1974 elections he stood as the head of the Social Equality List, which did not win a seat.

Ha-Olam ha-Zeh — New Force. During the term of the Seventh Knesset, it split into Meri — Israel Radical Camp and Israel Democrats — Black Panthers, neither of which won a seat in 1974. 143

activities in the administered areas not required for security reasons and called for peace initiatives. But at its Sixth Convention, at the end of December 1972, the majority rejected a proposal to leave the Alignment.

As the term of the Seventh Knesset drew to its close, the parties started preparing for the general election, due on 30 October. The Israel Labor Party decided that its Cabinet ministers should try to hammer out an agreed policy, and their conclusions, known as the "Galili Document," were approved by the Secretariat on 4 September by 78 votes to 0. The proposals provided for further Israel settlement in the areas, including the establishment of an urban center (but not a new port town) in the Rafa area, and measures for the rehabilitation and resettlement of Arab refugees, but did not involve any change in the legal status of the territories or in the citizenship of their inhabitants.

A re-alignment at the other end of the political spectrum was sparked by the retirement from regular army service of Major-General Ariel ("Arik") Sharon. Sharon, who joined the Liberal Party, immediately started a campaign for the expansion of Gaḥal into a broader union, which would present itself to the electorate as an alternative to the Labor-Mapam Alignment. Agreement was reached with the Free Center, which had broken away from Ḥerut early in 1967, the National ("Mamlakhti") List, and a section of the Land of Israel Movement to establish a new grouping, to be called Likkud ("Union").

There were also attempts to form an alignment on the left wing. Part of Siaḥ (*Semol Yisre'eli Hadash*—Israel New Left), a breakaway group from Mapam and most of Maki, led by its veteran leader Shmuel Mikunis, combined to form Moked ("Focus"), headed by Meir Pa'il.

The election campaign was rudely interrupted, however, by the sudden outbreak of war on Yom Kippur, 6 Oct. By common consent, all election propaganda was halted. The Central Elections Committee announced that, in view of the widespread mobilization, it would be impossible to hold the elections on the statutory date and the Knesset passed an amendment to the Knesset and Local Authorities Elections Law deferring the elections to 31 Dec.

When the election campaign restarted, it was on entirely different lines from those of the pre-war period. The Likkud declared that the Government had committed appalling blunders by failing to mobilize the reserves and move the armor up to the front in time to meet the Arab assault. They accused the Alignment, particularly Prime Minister Golda Meir and Defense Minister Moshe Dayan, of having left the armed forces unprepared for the emergency and demanded the Government's immediate resignation. The Cabinet resolved on an appointment of an enquiry commission, to be nominated by the President of the Supreme Court.

Left-wing circles inside and outside the Alignment also criticized Government policy before the war on the ground that it had been lacking in flexibility and initiative in pursuing the possibility of peace and that the policy of Jewish settlement in the Israel-held areas, as embodied, e.g., in the "Galili Document," had contributed to pushing the Arabs into war.

Mrs. Meir demanded that the party adopt clear-cut decisions on its post-war policy and a program was adopted which focused on efforts to achieve, at the forthcoming Geneva Peace Conference, a peace settlement which should ensure "defensible borders based on a territorial compromise" and "the preservation of the Jewish character of the State of Israel," which implied non-annexation of large areas inhabited by Arabs.

Likkud denounced the new Alignment program as leading to "surrender and endangering the nation's survival." While its spokesmen expressed readiness to consider territorial compromise with Egypt over the future of Sinai, they vigorously opposed "the renewed partition of the Land of Israel"—i.e., withdrawal from any part of Judea and Samaria (the "West Bank").

The National Religious Party had adopted a similar policy, 145 based on religious grounds, at its Convention in March, when it had also resolved to demand the amendment of the Law of Return (Amendment No. 2) 1970 (see EJYB 1973, pp. 248 and 307) to recognize only conversions to Judaism carried out according to the *halakhah*.

The votes were cast in over 4,000 polling stations for civilians and 1,500 for soldiers on active service, from Mount Hermon in the north to the port of Adabiya on the Gulf of Suez. An unprecedented feature was the high percentage of army votes. Outstanding features of the results (see Table) were a drop in the representatives of the Labor-Mapam Alignment to 51 seats and the gains by Likud (see Table).

The negotiations for the formation of a new coalition were prolonged. Mrs. Golda Meir, as the nominee of the largest party, the Labor-Mapam Alignment (which was reinforced by adhesion of three Arab members), was entrusted with the task by President Katzir. The NRP presented three demands as a condition for joining the coalition: the establishment of a national emergency government including the Likud; amendment of the law to recognize only conversions carried out according to the *halakhah;* and an understanding that, in negotiations with the Arab countries, Israel would not give up any part of the historic Land of Israel (Judea and Samaria). The Alignment rejected the first demand on the ground that there was no common basis of policy with the Likud, especially on the question of peace negotiations with the Arabs. As to the second, it was agreed that a cabinet committee should be given a year to find an agreed solution, and in the meantime the minister of the interior would not register as a Jew anyone not so recognized by the *halakhah.* It was also agreed that the government could enter into peace negotiations with Jordan, but no settlement involving withdrawal from part of Judea and Samaria would be ratified without a new general election. A strong minority in the NRP (mainly its youth faction), however, was opposed to joining the coalition on these terms and the

Chief Rabbinate, when approached for a halakhic opinion, did not sanction the NRP's participation.

Mrs. Meir also had trouble in her own party, in which there was dissension between "hawks" and "doves," opposition to Defense Minister Moshe Dayan, and some support, especially from the ex-Rafi faction, for the establishment of a national unity government. Dayan announced that, in view of the lack of support for him in the party, he would refuse to join the new cabinet, and his ex-Rafi colleague, Shimon Peres, did likewise. Mrs. Meir announced that she would return her mandate to the President. Intense efforts were made to persuade her to change her mind and the Labor Party's central council also called on Dayan and Peres to accept their posts in the cabinet.

The turning point came after a cabinet session at which intelligence reports of a possible renewal of hostilities by Syria were submitted. Dayan and Peres announced that, in order to avoid a continued cabinet crisis at such a time, they would agree to serve, the NRP decided, by a majority, to join the coalition, and Mrs. Meir rapidly completed her new cabinet. It was presented to the Knesset on March 10, 1974 and received a vote of confidence by 62 votes to 46, with 9 abstentions.

Israel Cabinets 1974

	Cabinet installed	
	March 10, 1974[1]	June 3, 1974[2]
Prime Minister	Golda Meir (Alignment)	Yitzhak Rabin (Alignment)
Deputy Prime Minister	Yigal Allon (")	Yigal Allon (")
Agriculture	Hayyim Gvati (")	Aharon Uzan (")
Commerce, Industry and Development	Haim Bar-Lev (")	Haim Bar-Lev (")
Communications	Aharon Uzan (")	Yitzhak Rabin[3] (")
Defense	Moshe Dayan (")	Shimon Peres (")
Education	Yigal Allon (")	Aharon Yadlin (")
Finance	Pinhas Sapir (")	Yehoshua Rabinowitz (")
Foreign Affairs	Abba Eban (")	Yigal Allon (")
Health	Victor Shemtov (")	Victor Shemtov (")
Housing	Yehoshua Rabinowitz (")	Avraham Ofer (")
Immigrant Absorption	Shelomo Rosen (")	Shelomo Rosen (")
Information	Shimon Peres (")	Aharon Yariv (")
Interior	Yosef Burg (NRP)	Shelomo Hillel[3] (")
Justice	Hayyim Zadok (Alignment)	Hayyim Zadok (")
Labor	Yitzhak Rabin (")	Moshe Baram (")

Religious Affairs	Yitzhak Raphael (NRP)	Hayyim Zadok[3] (")
Social Welfare	Michael Ḥazani (NRP)	Victor Shemtov[3] (")
Tourism	Moshe Kol (ILP)	Moshe Kol (ILP)
Transport	Aharon Yariv (Alignment)	Gad Ya'akobi (Alignment)
Without Portfolio	Israel Galili (")	Israel Galili (")
	Gideon Hausner (ILP)	Gideon Hausner (ILP)
		Shulamit Aloni (CRM)

[1] Following public criticism and demands for the resignation of Defense Minister Moshe Dayan after the publication of the partial report of the Agranat Commission on the background to the Yom Kippur War, Prime Minister Golda Meir submitted her resignation on April 11.

[2] Yitzḥak Rabin who was elected by the Israel Labor Party's Central Council as its candidate for the premiership on 22 April (receiving 56% of the votes as against Shimon Peres, the only other candidate) was entrusted by the President with the task of forming a new cabinet. His cabinet was installed on 3 June after receiving a vote of confidence by 61 votes to 51, with 5 abstentions.

[3] "Pro tempore"

2 WOMEN IN PUBLIC LIFE

Jewish women began to take an active part in public and communal life in the new *yishuv* early in the 20th century. In the summer of 1914 a handful of young women from the Second Aliyah met in Merḥavyah and established Moʿeẓet ha-Poʿalot (Council of Working Women), the first women's organization in the country. The Council provided agricultural training for women to prepare them for working on the land alongside the men. They joined in debates on public issues and left no doubt about their desire and ability for responsible citizenship. Significantly, there was no opposition from the men, in Ha-Shomer, in the Teachers' Association, and in the kibbutzim women enjoyed full equality from the very beginning. They participated in the *yishuv's* public bodies since the 1920 elections to its "parliament," Asefat ha-Nivḥarim, when they were given the vote despite objections from extreme religious groups.

Since educational opportunities are the same for girls and boys, except in yeshivot, women are to be found in all institutes of higher learning, as both students and teachers. The number of women in the Knesset has fluctuated between eight and ten. Golda Meir as prime minister is Israel's best known woman but others have been prominent in all fields of culture and artistic endeavors. Women's organizations representing every shade of opinion, as well as non-party bodies, do important work in social service, running creches, kindergartens, clubs, etc.: examples are Moʿeẓet ha-Poʿalot, WIZO and associations affiliated to the Mizrachi (NRP), the Liberal Party, and others.

Women have played their role in the defense of the country. Three thousand volunteers served during World

Prime Minister Golda Meir inspects a guard of honor of the Women's Corps ("Ḥen") of the Israel Defense Forces, at Lydda, 1969. Courtesy Government Press Office, Tel Aviv.

War II with the British army ATS and WAAF. Hannah Szenes and two other women were parachuted into occupied Europe. Girls served in the Palmaḥ and the Israel Defense Forces. There is a difference, however, in the Israel army's recognition of women's special characteristics: they do not fight. Most perform clerical, medical, housekeeping, and communications duties. Some pack parachutes, teach, or do cultural work in development areas. Unmarried women from 18 to 26 are conscripted for 20 months. Orthodox girls with scruples about army service are exempt.

For legal status of women see, *Society*, Israel Pocket Library Series.

3 ARABS AND DRUZE

The Proclamation of Independence promised that Israel would maintain "complete equality of social and political rights for all its citizens without distinction of creed, race or sex" and called on the Arabs in Israel "to play their part in building the state on the basis of full and equal citizenship and due representation in all its institutions." Israel has carried out these pledges in so far as possible in a country under constant siege and menace by the surrounding Arab peoples.

At the end of 1973 Israel had some 430,000 Arab and Druze citizens, as well as some 70,000 in Jerusalem who enjoy the rights of permanent residents but retain Jordanian citizenship of their own choice. All the citizens receive the parliamentary franchise at the age of 18 (Israel was the first country in the Middle East to give the vote to Arab women) and permanent residents, even if not citizens, have the right to vote at local authority elections. They enjoy equality before the law. Arabic, which is one of Israel's two official languages, may be used in Parliament and in the courts, and in approaches to the authorities. Stamps, coins, and banknotes bear Arabic inscriptions. Summaries of Supreme Court decisions are issued in Arabic for Arab lawyers.

In view of the state of war still maintained by Israel's Arab neighbors, Israel Arabs are sometimes torn between loyalty to their country and their Arab affiliations, but there is a growing pattern of coexistence between them and their Jewish fellow-citizens. Arabs are exempt from military service, to avoid any conflict of conscience, but Druze and Circassians are liable for conscription at the request of

Faris Fcillah, the first Druze judge in Israel, being sworn in by President Shazar, October 1968. Courtesy Government Press Office, Tel Aviv.

these communities themselves. Many Beduin also serve in the armed forces. Military government, which involved restrictions on movement in and out of border areas, mainly inhabited by Arabs, for security reasons, was gradually curtailed as security improved and abolished in 1966.

National Politics. The Arab community plays a full and active role in national politics. Except for the first Knesset election in 1949, the proportion of Arab voters has been higher than that among the Jews. Table 1 shows the comparison. After the first Knesset, which had only three Arab members, there have generally been seven and sometimes eight (Second, Third, and Fifth Knessets). Most of these—two in the First Knesset, five in the Second, Third, and Fourth, four in the Fifth, and Sixth, five in the Seventh and four in the Eighth. One of these died two months after the elections and his place was taken by the next on the list, who was a Jew—have been members of lists associated with, or affiliated to, Mapai (since 1968 the Israel Labor

153

Party) or its alliances with other parties. These lists, which have names like Cooperation and Fraternity or Progress and Development, are generally divided along religious, geographical, and family lines. While the percentage voting for Mapai (Labor) or its affiliated lists dropped from more than 60% in 1949 to 50% in 1965, it nevertheless remained greater than that of any other party and rose to 57% in 1969 for the Labor-Mapam alliance (Ma'arakh). In 1973, however, after the rise in Arab national sentiment that followed the Yom Kippur War, it fell to 44.6%.

The Israel Communist Party tried to attract Arab votes by making an Arab nationalist appeal, and provided a legal way of opposing the regime. This was particularly true of Rakaḥ (New Communist List), the larger of the two factions into which the party split in 1965—the smaller, Maki, being mainly Jewish. Rakaḥ succeeded, together with Mapam, in gaining control of the Nazareth municipal council for a short period, from December 1965 to March 1966 and thereafter remained a strong opposition. The strength of the Communists in the Knesset elections has been irregular; winning 22% of the Arab vote in 1949 they dropped to 10% by 1959 but went up again to 22.6% in 1965, when they secured 38,800 votes (of which 38,000 went to Rakaḥ), as compared with the labor affiliated lists' total of 48,000. In 1969 Rakaḥ obtained 34,000 votes to 67,000 for the Ma'arakh and its affiliated lists and in 1973 it obtained almost 50,000 (36.9%).

Mapam, the third of the national parties to appeal to the Arabs on a sustained basis, always included an Arab candidate in a prominent place on its list. Its strength gradually increased to 12.5% of the Arab vote in 1959 and fell slightly to 9.2% in 1965, after which it joined the Ma'arakh.

Table 2 shows how the Arab vote has been divided between the main parties and Table 3 gives the results in 1973.

Local Government. The Ministry of the Interior has strongly encouraged the formation of local councils in order to raise the level of Arab local government to that of the Jews, to serve as a link between the villages and the government, and to act as a vehicle for economic progress, as part of the program for rural development. In 1948 only three Arab localities under Israel rule were governed by local councils. The municipal council of Nazareth was established in 1935 and that of Shepharam in 1934, while the village council of Kafr Yasīf dates back to 1925. By 1973 there were two Arab municipalities, 47 villages with local councils, and another 27 within larger regional councils. These covered some 83% of Israel's Arabs. Participation in

Table 1. Percentage of Electors Voting at National Elections, Jews and Arabs, 1949–73

Election Year	Arabs	Jews
1949	79.3	86.9
1951	85.5	75.1
1955	91.0	82.8
1959	88.9	81.6
1961	85.6	81.6
1965	87.8	83.0
1969	84.0	82.0
1973	80.0	78.6

Table 2. Votes Cast in Arab and Druze Districts, 1949–60

Election Year	Mapai (Labor) and affiliated lists	Communists	Mapam	Others
1949	61.3	22.2	0.2	16.3
1951	66.5	16.3	5.6	11.6
1955	62.4	15.6	7.3	14.7
1959	52.0	10.0	12.5	25.5
1961	50.8	22.7	11.0	15.5
1965	50.1	22.6[1]	9.2	18.1
1969	57.3[2]	29.7[3]	—[2]	13.0

[1] Rakaḥ + Maki.
[2] Labor-Mapam Alliance (Ma'arakh).
[3] Rakaḥ—29.1%; Maki—0.6%.

Table 3. Votes Cast in Arab and Druze Districts, 1973

	Votes	Percentages
Votes cast	140,349	
Valid votes cast	134,330	100
Labor-Mapam Alignment	16,641	12.4
Beduin and Villagers (affiliated to Alignment)	14,703	11.0
Cooperation and Fraternity (affiliated to Alignment)	7,395	5.5
Progress and Development (affiliated to Alignment)	21,044	15.7
Total Alignment and affiliated lists	69,683	44.6
Rakah (New Communist List)	49,611	36.9
Likkud (Gaḥal and others)	4,570	3.4
Israel Arabs (associated with Likkud)	2,251	1.6
National Religious Party	10,471	7.8
Others	7,644	5.7

The total number of eligible voters was 174,938.

local elections, which has been larger than that of either Jews or Arabs in national elections, bears witness to the close relationship between the council and the villagers. Generally the national parties only vie for council seats in the larger localities, such as Nazareth; in the smaller villages the candidates generally represent rival families, clans, or religious communities. The major part of the councils' budgets is raised by local taxes, calculated according to the area of land or number of rooms owned, but the government makes substantial contributions, especially for development projects, like the installation of electricity and water lines, or the construction of roads and schools, to which it usually contributes about 50% of the total expenditure.

Administered Areas. In keeping with the cease-fire
agreements and the provisions of international law, the areas

occupied by the Israel Defense Forces as a result of the defeat of the Arab armies in 1967 and 1973 are under military government until a settlement, which will determine the political future of the areas, is attained by agreement with the neighboring Arab countries.

While the military governor in each area is responsible for civilian services, as well as security, local affairs are administered, as far as possible, by the Arab population through existing bodies, such as municipalities and police. Thus, in the two most populated areas—Judea and Samaria (the "West Bank") and the Gaza Strip, there are only some 500 Israel officials compared with 12,500 local personnel. The officials in charge of civilian activities are seconded from, and work with, the corresponding Israel Ministries, but are themselves directly under the command of the military governors.

Major problems of policy are dealt with by two governmental committees: a cabinet committee coordinates all work in the areas, particularly that of a political or security nature; a committee of directors-general of government ministries concerns itself with civilian and economic problems. Decisions affecting policy in the areas are made by the Government and carried out by the Ministry of Defense and the General Staff, so that a consistent policy and direct control by the supreme civilian jurisdiction are assured.

There are 23 municipalities and 31 rural councils in Judea and Samaria, and three municipalities and seven rural councils in the Gaza Strip and North Sinai. Liaison officers of the Israel Ministry of the Interior approve their budgets, arrange to lend them funds at low interest, and audit their finances and administration. Municipal elections were held in Judea and Samaria in 1972, in accordance with Jordanian law. Candidates were given time on Israel television and the election campaign was lively. Seventy-five percent of the voters participated and, as a result of the elections, about half the mayors were replaced by new ones.

4 COMMUNICATIONS MEDIA

The Press. The first Hebrew newspapers in Erez Israel, *Ha-Levanon* and *Ḥavaẓẓelet*, were established as weeklies in 1863 by founders of the first Hebrew printing presses in Jerusalem. They differed from the Hebrew periodicals that had already begun to appear in Europe in that news and current events were central and the language was livelier and simpler, avoiding much of the artificiality of the Diaspora style. Eventually the Jerusalem papers exerted considerable influence on the early stages of the revival of spoken Hebrew.

Both papers were closed down by the Turkish authorities within a year, but *Ḥavaẓẓelet* was reopened in 1870 and continued to appear until 1911. It attracted many writers, among whom was Eliezer Ben-Yehuda, the pioneer of modern spoken Hebrew. Ben-Yehuda was responsible for many literary and linguistic improvements, but he wanted to produce a newspaper in the spirit of the new Jewish community. In 1884 he broke away to found *Ha-Ẓevi*, which breathed a new spirit into Hebrew journalism. In 1900, following difficulties with the authorities, the name of his paper was changed to *Hashkafah* which from 1904 appeared biweekly. It was Ben-Yehuda who published the first daily, *Ha-Or* (1910), in which his son, Ittamar Ben-Avi, was one of the leading editors. This paper introduced technical innovations, such as the more prominent use of headlines, and lasted until 1915.

The major changes in the country's life brought about by the Second Aliyah (1905–1914) were not reflected in Ben-Yehuda's papers, and the newcomers established their own organs. In 1907 they founded the weekly *Ha-Po'e ha-Ẓa'ir*, as well as a Yiddish weekly, *Anfang* (which, in 1910, was replaced by another Hebrew journal called *Ha-Aḥdut*). These papers, the first of the organized labor movement, opposed many of the ideas of Ben-Yehuda and also sought to eliminate the pathos which characterized some of the writing in his paper. Papers began to proliferate in Jerusalem. Among the newcomers was *Ha-Ḥerut* (1909), edited by Abraham Elmaleh, which had a large Sephardi readership. For a time it was a daily, and was the only Hebrew newspaper to continue being published throughout World War I (up to 1917).

After World War I, the press underwent a process of modernization. A number of daily papers made their appearance, and a clear distinction emerged between the dailies and the weeklies. The latter no longer gave straight news, placing their emphasis on signed articles. The daily papers that now appeared devoted themselves to topical material and could not specialize; this left room for the development of professional periodicals. A further postwar innovation was the introduction of afternoon papers, generally of a more popular nature than the morning press, as well as a variety of illustrated weeklies. A further consequence now was the clearer distinction between the writer and the journalist; hitherto the dividing line had been blurred but now there emerged the journalist-reporter type, familiar in Western journalism. The important dailies engaged in general publishing. Coverage of literary, scientific, and artistic developments tended to be concentrated in the Friday supplement, which became a regular feature of most papers (the Friday paper being the weekend issue as no papers appear on Saturday). The post-World-War-I period was also marked by a move away from Jerusalem to Tel Aviv, which became the center of newspaper publishing.

Ḥadshot ha-Areẓ (later *Haaretz*) began to appear in 1919. In 1923 Moshe Gluecksohn took over the chief editorship and gave the paper its distinctive character. In 1937 it was bought by Salman Schocken, who appointed his son

Gershom Schocken as editor. From 1951 it produced a weekly children's paper called *Haarez Shellanu.*

Initially, Ben-Yehuda worked for *Ḥadshot ha-Arez,* but when he realized that its policies differed from his own, he found *Do'ar ha-Yom* (1919), edited by his son Ittamar Ben-Avi, which continued to appear in Jerusalem for 18 years. Until 1929, all daily papers made their appearance at

A Tel Aviv newspaper stand. Courtesy Government Press Office, Tel Aviv.

noon, Ben-Avi being the first to bring out his paper in the early morning. This was made possible in the first place by the inauguration of a direct news service to Palestine (until 1929 the agency reports were sent to Cairo and from there went by train, so that news in the papers was generally two days old).

In 1925 the labor movement decided to publish its own paper, *Davar,* which became the most widely circulated morning paper. The first editors were Berl Katznelson, Zalman Rubashov (Shazar), and Moshe Beilinson. From 1931 it produced a weekly children's magazine (*Davar li-Yladim*). The growth in the number of parties led to a parallel growth in the number of papers, as each party was interested in propagating its views through its own organ. Thus the Revisionists produced successively *Ha-Am, Hazit ha-Am, Ha-Yarden,* and *Ha-Mashkif.* The Herut movement, founded in 1948, published *Herut. Ha-Boker,* supported by the General Zionists, reflected the views of the citrus growers, industrialists, and businessmen. *Herut* and *Ha-Boker* merged in 1966 under the name of *Ha-Yom,* which closed down in 1970. The Mizrachi parties published *Ha-Zofeh;* Agudat Israel, *Ha Yom* and *Ha-Kol;* and Po'alei Agudat Israel, *She'arim.* The left-wing parties' papers were *Mishmar* (later *Al ha-Mishmar*) and *La-Mer-hav* (the latter merged with *Davar* in 1971). The Communist daily was *Kol ha-Am,* which became a weekly in 1970.

The mid-1930s saw the introduction of afternoon papers. The early ventures were short-lived, some of them being afternoon editions of morning papers. In 1939 Ezriel Carlebach founded *Yedi'ot Aharonot;* after a disagreement he left this paper in 1947 and founded *Ma'ariv.* Apart from *Ha-Dor* (1949–55), published by Mapai, these two papers, both with considerable circulations, have remained the only afternoon papers (in fact, they appear in the late morning, with extra afternoon editions only if warranted by special news). These papers are characterized by a lighter presentation, short items, and prominent headlines. There are also *Hadshot Sport* (1960) and two dailies specializing in economic affairs: *Sha'ar* and *Yom-Yom* (both founded 1964).

Special attention has been given to papers for recent immigrants who have difficulty in reading the ordinary Hebrew press. Voweled newspapers began to appear in 1940, when *Davar* published *Hegeh*, with translations of difficult words into German. Since then a number of voweled papers for new immigrants have been published, notably *Omer* (a daily, published by the Histadrut from 1950). In addition, there is a considerable circulation for foreign-language newspapers. These include the English-language *Jerusalem Post* (founded by Gershon Agron as the *Palestine Post* in 1932), a daily which was of particular significance during the period of the British Mandate; the German-language *Jedioth Hadashoth* (1936), replaced by *Israel Nachrichten* (1974), *al-Yawm* (1948), replaced by *al-Anba* (1968), in Arabic and *al-Quds* (1968), in the same language, both published in Jerusalem: *Uj Kelet* (1948) in Hungarian: *L'Information* (1967) in French: *Israelskie Nowiny i Kurier* (1958) in Polish: *Letste Nayes* (1959) in Yiddish, the most widely circulated of the foreign-language papers: *Izraelski Far* in Bulgarian (1959): *Viata Noastra* (1959) in Rumanian: and *Nasha Strana* in Russian.

In 1973 there were 21 morning and 2 afternoon papers. *Davar* and *Haaretz* sold about 40,000 copies each, the other Hebrew papers between 5,000 and 18,000. The evening papers sold between 93,000 and 160,000. Sales of all papers are higher on Fridays than on other days. There are about 400 other publications, 70 of them under government auspices. Of these 50 appear weekly and 150 biweekly. Over 300 are in Hebrew and 50 in English.

A national news agency is provided by ITIM Associated Israel Press, which supplies coverage of Israel news to the local newspapers, as well as distributing Reuters and Agence France Presse dispatches.

Local papers and dispatches filed by foreign correspondents are subject to military censorship, which is confined, however, to security matters. Comment and political news are free from control. A censor's ruling can be appealed before a committee of three, representing the army, the newspaper editors and the public, which decides by a majority.

Broadcasting. Broadcasting was inaugurated in 1936 when the British Mandatory authorities started the Palestine Broadcasting Service. The programs were in English, Arabic, and Hebrew, and the studios were situated in Jerusalem. The following year saw the foundation of the Palestine Broadcasting Symphony Orchestra, whose weekly concerts became an important part of the Jerusalem musical scene.

During the last months of the Mandate, the Haganah maintained an illegal broadcasting station called Kol Israel (Voice of Israel). At the time of the establishment of the state (1948), Jerusalem was cut off, and only a skeleton service could be maintained there. The broadcasting center was established in Tel Aviv and Kol Israel's first legal program was a relay of the Declaration of Independence. Initially constituted as part of the Ministry of the Interior, Kol Israel was later transferred to the Prime Minister's Office. Early in 1950 the Jerusalem broadcasting center was reestablished and most of the departments transferred there, although studios continued to be maintained in Tel Aviv and later also in Haifa.

Although initially confined to a single wavelength, the broadcasting service gradually expanded to four simultaneous broadcasts. Network A, broadcasting in Hebrew, presents a variety of programs including news and current events, symphony concerts, plays, school broadcasts, and higher education. Network B, which broadcasts commercials, is a light program concentrating on entertainment and light music. For part of the time it broadcasts programs in non-Hebrew languages for new immigrants and tourists. It also has a daily program in simple Hebrew for listeners with a limited vocabulary. Network C is a shortwave service to other countries. It was originally founded in 1950 by the

World Zionist Organization as *Kol Zion la-Golah* ("The Voice of Zion to the Diaspora"), and was incorporated into Kol Israel's external services in 1959. It broadcasts in Hebrew, English, French, Yiddish, Russian, Hungarian, Rumanian, Ladino, Mograbi, and Persian. Network D broadcasts mainly in Arabic for Arabs in Israel, the Israel-held areas and other Middle Eastern countries. The only other broadcasting station inside Israel is *Gallei Zahal*, which is operated by the army.

In 1965 responsibility for broadcasting was removed from the Prime Minister's Office and vested in a Broadcasting Authority. Its Board of Directors and the Public Committee consist of public figures appointed by the President of the State on the advice of the government. The change was made to ensure greater autonomy in broadcasting policy and administration.

Radio has played a vital role in the country's educational, and cultural progress, as well as the provision of up-to-date information. Virtually every home has a radio and listening is extensive, especially to news programs. Although developing late, it made rapid strides in its production techniques, and its programs have received several international awards. Some of the country's leading cultural events (e.g., the annual Song Festival and the triennial International Bible Quiz) were originated and sponsored by the Israel Broadcasting Authority.

Television was late in coming to Israel. The delay was primarily due to an assessment of economic priorities which put television comparatively low on the list. The first break-through came when the Rothschild Foundation offered to finance classroom teaching on television through an open network. This was directed primarily to schools in development areas with large new immigrant populations and difficulties in obtaining teachers. A pilot project went into operation in 1965, which developed into a regular daily service.

Pressure for general television increased as a result of the presence in the country of tens of thousands of TV sets, mostly in areas populated by Arabs who were intensively watching programs from the neighboring Arab countries. The problem became even more acute as a result of the Six-Day War of 1967, after which it was decided to inaugurate general television. The transmission of programs in Hebrew and Arabic began in 1968 and rapidly attracted a wide and growing audience. At the beginning of 1974 programs were broadcast for some 6 hours a day: an hour for children (in Hebrew), $1\frac{1}{2}$ hours in Arabic, and $3\frac{1}{2}$ hours in Hebrew, as well as 3 hours on Saturday morning. The programs include news, which is most popular, foreign thrillers, feature films, local and foreign entertainment programs, discussions on current affairs, and documentaries.

Before elections, all parties participating are given a minimum period of free time on radio and TV: those represented in the Knesset receive more in proportion to their strengths. TV played a particularly important role during the Yom Kippur War and the subsequent election campaign.

5 RELIGION AND THE STATE

In the days of Ottoman rule, religious adherence in the Holy Land had far-reaching implications for communal and even national identity. Since Islam drew no distinction between "church" and state (the latter having both political and religious functions), the Muslims saw no reason to organize as a community. They felt that they were the state, and the government should put their needs first. It was the non-Muslims who needed recognized communal organizations, enjoying internal autonomy, to protect their interests. The Ottoman authorities thus recognized a number of Christian communities, known as *millets*, led by patriarchs, who were both their high priests and ethnarchs. This system was maintained by the British Mandatory administration and in independent Israel religious freedom includes not only the right of each religious community to observe its own weekly rest days and festivals, but also the preservation of the jurisdiction of their religious courts in certain matters of personal status, such as marriage, divorce, and inheritance.

Among the Jewish community, the place of religion in public life is rooted in centuries of tradition and is influenced by its central role in the national culture and the preservation of the Jewish people in exile. In independent Israel, the relationship between religious practice, national goals, and individual freedom is an issue of crucial importance and has given rise to deep feeling and prolonged controversy.

The Chief Rabbinate. Under Turkish rule, religious and judicial authority in the Jewish community were vested in the ḥakham bashi (chief rabbi) of Jerusalem, also entitled *rishon le-Zion* ("first in Zion"), who was

Electoral assembly for the Chief Rabbinate. Seated in the front row (left to right) are Rabbi Ovadiah Yosef and Rabbi Shlomo Goren, elected Sephardi and Ashkenazi chief rabbis respectively and the two incumbents Rabbi Isaac Nissim and Rabbi Isser Yehuda Unterman. (1972.) (G.P.O., Tel Aviv)

elected by the leaders of the local Sephardi community. The Ashkenazim conducted their own rabbinical courts, the president of the Jerusalem *bet din* being regarded without a formal appointment, as head of their community.

In 1920 the first British high commissioner, Sir Herbert Samuel, appointed a committee to consider the creation of a united Chief Rabbinate for the entire country. It recommended that a board of electors, consisting of officiating rabbis and laymen, elect a Chief Rabbinate Council, with Sephardi and Ashkenazi chief rabbis as joint presidents, three Sephardi and three Ashkenazi rabbis as members, and three laymen in an advisory capacity.

In 1921 the electors assembled in Jerusalem and elected the council, with R. Abraham Isaac Kook and R. Ya'akov Meir as chief rabbis. (The Sephardi chief rabbi retained the title of *rishon le-Zion*.) The government recog- 167 nized the council and any *bet din* sanctioned by it as "the sole authorities in matters of Jewish Law" and undertook to execute through civil courts judgments given by its *bet din*.

In 1922 the jurisdiction of the Chief Rabbinate was defined by Order-in-Council. Section 53 of the order stipulated: "The Rabbinical Courts of the Jewish Community shall have: (a) exclusive jurisdiction in matters of marriage and divorce, alimony and confirmation of wills of members of their community other than foreigners . . . (b) Jurisdiction in any other matter of personal status of such persons, where all the parties to the action consent to their jurisdiction. (c) Exclusive jurisdiction over any case as to the constitution or internal administration of a Wakf or religious endowment constituted before the Rabbinical Courts according to Jewish Law." In 1928, when the government finally approved the Regulations of the Jewish Community Keneset Yisrael, the Chief Rabbinate Council was recognized by it as the supreme religious body of the Jewish community.

The Chief Rabbinate Council was enlarged by the co-option of a number of renowned religious scholars. The first incumbents were succeeded by Chief Rabbis Isaac Halevi Herzog (1936–59) and Ben-Zion Meir Ḥai Ouziel (1939–54). During their tenure, relations with the lay authorities were harmonious and fruitful. R. Herzog played a leading role in the relations between the Jewish population and the Mandatory government. He frequently appeared on behalf of the *yishuv* before the high commissioner and the various commissions appointed to investigate the situation in Palestine. Together with his colleague, R. Ouziel, he initiated cooperation between scientists and rabbis in seeking technological solutions to halakhic problems.

Sephardi Chief Rabbi Ouziel died in 1954, and in 1955 Rabbi Yiẓḥak Nissim was elected *rishon le-Zion* and Sephardi chief rabbi. In 1963, after the death of Ashkenazi Chief Rabbi Herzog, R. Issar Yehudah Unterman was elected Ashkenazi chief rabbi and Chief Rabbi Nissim was reelected. In 1973 Rabbis Shlomo Goren and Ovadia Yosef were elected Ashkenazi and Sephardi chief rabbis respectively.

The Chief Rabbinical Council has departments for *kashrut*, supervision of scribes (*soferim*), and committees for marriage licenses; confirmation of rabbinical ordination (*semikhah*); precepts specific to the Holy Land; and responsa on matters of *halakhah*. The chief rabbis preside over the *Bet Din Gadol* (Rabbinical Supreme Court), which hears appeals from decisions of the district rabbinical courts.

Religion in the State of Israel. The Declaration of Independence states: "The State of Israel . . . will maintain complete equality of social and political rights for all its citizens, without distinction of creed, race or sex. It will guarantee freedom of religion and conscience, of language, education and culture. It will safeguard the Holy Places of all religions . . ."

Article 2 of the first regular government's statement of Basic Principles, presented to the Knesset on March 8, 1949, reads:

The state will provide for the public religious needs of its inhabitants but will prevent coercion in matters of religion. The Sabbath and the Jewish holy days will be fixed days of rest in the State of Israel. The right of non-Jews to their Sabbath and days of rest will be safeguarded.

These principles were restated and rephrased by later governments. From 1959 they were supplemented by the obligation to "guarantee religious education to all children whose parents so desire" and to "maintain the status quo in the state in religious matters," thus confirming an unwritten agreement which had been in force since the establishment of independence.

The powers of the Mandatory high commisioner in matters of religion are now exercised by the minister of religious affairs, who is responsible for the administrative aspects of the Chief Rabbinate and the rabbinical courts, the religious councils and religious committees, and the appointment and maintenance of local rabbis. The ministry deals with *kashrut*, yeshivot, synagogues, *mikva'ot*, the supervision of burials, and the provision of ritual appurtenances and sacred books. It also provides religious services for Karaites and Samaritans, Muslims, Christians, and Druze.

Under the Religious Services Budget Law (1967) every local authority is required to appoint a religious council consisting of religious individuals that will provide all public religious facilities for the local population. The composition of each religious council must be ratified by the minister of religious affairs. Forty-five percent of the members are nominated by the minister, 45% by the local authority, and 10% by the local rabbinate. Any deficits in the operation of the religious council are covered by the local authority (two-thirds) and the government (one-third). In 1972, 190 such councils were in existence.

One of the first legislative acts of the Provisional State Council after independence was aimed at safeguarding the social aspect of Sabbath and festivals throughout the country. This was the Days of Rest Ordinance of June 3, 1948, which prescribed the Sabbath and the Jewish festivals as regular days of rest, while assuring non-Jews of the right to observe their own Sabbath and festivals.

The Hours of Work and Rest Law of 1951 grants every employee at least 36 continuous hours of leisure each week. For Jews this weekly rest period coincides with the Sabbath, and a similar rest is prescribed on the Jewish festivals. This law, however, does not cover cafés, the self-employed, or cooperative enterprises, including public transport. These are regulated by municipal ordinances.

The law grants the minister of labor authority to permit work on the Sabbath in enterprises regarded as vital to national security or the economy, or installations like blast furnaces or cement kilns which require continuous operation. The issue of licenses to work on Sabbath is subject to approval by a committee consisting of the prime minister, the minister of religious affairs, and the minister of labor.

In 1953 the Knesset passed the Rabbinical Courts Jurisdiction (Marriage and Divorce) Law, which gave the Chief Rabbinate and the religious courts exclusive jurisdiction of all matrimonial cases, including alimony and support of children, for all Jewish residents, including foreign nationals. Jews may marry only by the traditional ceremony *(huppah ve-kiddushin)* after the marriage has been duly registered with the rabbinate, and only rabbis approved by the Chief Rabbinate may conduct marriage ceremonies. Rabbinical courts also have jurisdiction in matters of trusteeship, confirmation of wills, etc., where the parties involved accept their authority. Attempts have been made to legalize civil marriages by appeals to the High Court of Justice, and some people get around the law by civil marriage abroad (particularly in nearby Cyprus). A certain status has, however, been accorded by law to "common law wives." Rabbinical judges *(dayyanim)*, who have the same status as judges of district courts, are appointed by the president of the state on the recommendation of a special committee and take the oath of allegiance in his presence.

Controversies have flared up from time to time over the application of religious laws and principles to matters in the public domain, such as religious education, Sabbath observance, and *Kashrut*. The most prolonged controversy has been that over the question of "Who is a Jew?" i.e., how should Jewish nationality *(le'om)* be defined for the purpose of the population register? (See Political Life and Parties, above.)

See also *Religious Life*, Israel Pocket Library Series.

GLOSSARY

Aliyah, (1) immigration to Erez Israel; (2) one of the waves of immigration to Erez Israel from the early 1880s.

Asefat ha-Nivḥarim, representative assembly elected by Jews in Palestine during the period of the British Mandate (1920–48).

Ashkenazi (pl. **Ashkenazim**), German or West-, Central-, or East-European Jew(s), as contrasted with Sephardi(m).

Bilu, first modern movement for pioneering and agricultural settlement in Erez Israel, founded in 1882 at Kharkov, Russia.

Diaspora, Jews living in the "dispersion" outside Erez Israel; area of Jewish settlement outside Erez Israel.

Erez Israel, Land of Israel; Palestine.

Haganah, clandestine Jewish organization for armed self-defense in Erez Israel under the British Mandate, which eventually evolved into a people's militia and became the basis for the Israel army.

Histadrut (abbr. for Heb. **Ha-Histadrut ha-Kelalit shel ha-Ovedim ha-Ivriyyim be-Erez Israel).** Erez Israel Jewish Labor Federation, founded in 1920; subsequently renamed Histadrut ha-Ovedim be-Erez Israel.

Holocaust, the organized mass persecution and annihilation of European Jewry by the Nazis (1933–1945).

Kibbutz (pl. **kibbutzim**), larger-size commune constituting a settlement in Erez Israel based mainly on agriculture but engaging also in industry.

Knesset, parliament of the State of Israel.

Leḥi (abbr. for Heb. **Loḥamei Ḥerut Israel,** "Fighters for the Freedom of Israel" also L.Ḥ.Y), radically anti-British armed underground organization in Palestine, founded in 1940 by dissidents from I.Z.L.

Mandate, Palestine, responsibility for the administration of Palestine conferred on Britain by the League of Nations in 1922; mandatory government: the British administration of Palestine.

Moshav, smallholders' cooperative agricultural settlement in Israel.

Moshavah, earliest type of Jewish village in modern Erez Israel in which farming is conducted on individual farms mostly on privately owned land.

War of Independence, war of 1947–49 when the Jews of Israel fought off Arab invading armies and ensured the establishment of the new State.

Yeshivah, Jewish traditional academy devoted primarily to study of rabbinic literature.

Yishuv, settlement; more specifically, the Jewish community of Erez Israel in the pre-State period. The pre-Zionist community is generally designated the "old yishuv" and the community evolving from 1880, the "new yishuv."

BIBLIOGRAPHY

GOVERNANCE: BEFORE STATE. G. Young, *Corps de droit Otto-man*, 7 vols. (1905–06).

E. Samuel, in: JJSO, 2 (1960), 219–35.

A. Heidborn, *Manuel de droit public et administratif de l'Empire Ottoman*, 2 vols. (1908–12).

Palestine, Municipal Tax Commission for Jerusalem *Report* (1920).

Palestine, Committee on Village Administration and Responsibility *Report* (1941).

Great Britain, Colonial Office, *Annual Reports to the League of Nations* (1922–).

A Survey of Palestine Prepared in December 1945 and January 1946 for the Information of the Anglo-American Committee of Inquiry, 2 vols. (1946).

R. H. Drayton, *Laws of Palestine in Force on the 31st Day of December, 1933*, 3 vols. (1934).

E. Samuel, *British Traditions in the Administration of Israel* (1957).

M. Attias (ed.), *Sefer ha-Te'udot shel ha-Va'ad ha-Le'ummi . . . 1918–1948* (1963²).

LOCAL GOVERNMENT. M. Gurion (Wager), *Mavo le-Toledot ha-Shilton ha-Mekomi be-Yisrael* (1956/57).

A Kidron, *Ha-Shilton ha-Mekomi bi-Medinat Yisrael* (1954).

D. Luzki, *Ha-Shilton ha-Mekomi be-Yisrael* (1958).

INSTITUTIONS AND INSTRUMENTS OF STATE. E. Rackman, *Israel's Emerging Constitution, 1948–1951* (1955).

M. S. Bernstein, *The Politics of Israel* (1957).

O. Kraines, *Government and Politics in Israel* (1961).

L. G. Seligman, *Leadership in a New Nation* (1964).

Y. Freudenheim, *Government in Israel* (1967).

L. Fein, *Politics in Israel* (1968).

A. Arian, *Ideological Change in Israel* (1968).

Klinghoffer, in: *Das Oeffentliche Recht der Gegenwart*, 14 (1965), 427–541.

M. Burstein, *Self-government of the Jews in Palestine since 1900* (1934).

A. Revusky, *Jews in Palestine* (1945²).

ESCO Foundation, *Palestine, A Study of Jewish, Arab and British Policies,* 2 vols. (1947), index.

M. Attias, *Knesset Yisrael be-Erez Yisrael* (1944).

A. Zidon, *Knesset, the Parliament of Israel* (1967).

L. J. Fein, *Politics in Israel* (1967).

H. Merhavia, *Am u-Moledet* (1948), chs. 3, 5, 11.

M. Shemueli, *Perakim be-Toledot ha-Ziyyonut u-Tenu'at ha-Avodah,* 3, 4 (1955–58), index.

Haaretz, *Miflagot be-Yisrael Erev ha-Beḥirot la-Knesset ha-Sheniyyah* (1951).

A. Ziv, *Eser ha-Shanim ha-Rishonot 1948–1958* (1958).

S. Shiḥor, *1958–1961: Yoman Eru'ei Shalosh Shanim* (1961).

H. Smith, *Ha-Kol al ha-Beḥirot be-Yisrael* (1969).

M. Rosetti, *Knesset: its Origin, Forms, and Procedure* (1966).

W. Eytan, *The First Ten Years* (1958), 191–212.

Israel, Misrad ha-Ḥuz, *Sekirah,* supplement to foreign minister's budget speech (1965–   ).

Government Year Book, 1950–

H. E. Baker, *The Legal System of Israel* (1968).

Y. Allon, *The Making of Israel's Army* (1969).

idem, *Shield of David* (1970).

S. Peres, *David's Sling* (1970).

State Comptroller's Law, 5718–1958 (consolidated version).

Israel, State Comptroller's Office, *Annual Reports,* (1952–   ).

State Comptroller of Israel and his Office at Work (1963), publ. by State Comptroller's Office.

L. Boim, *Mosad ha-Ombudsman* (1965).

JJSO   *Jewish Journal of Sociology* (1959 ff.).
EJYB   *Encyclopaedia Judaica Year Book.*

INDEX